Trees and Woodland
in the
British Landscape

The Earl's Colne Map, dated 1598. Tracing after the original in Essex Record Office. *See* pp. 112, 143, 167 and 189, reference 51.

Archaeology in the Field Series

Trees and Woodland in the British Landscape

Oliver Rackham

London

J. M. Dent & Sons Ltd

First published 1976
© Text and line illustrations, Oliver Rackham, 1976

Made in Great Britain
at the
Aldine Press, Letchworth, Herts
for
J. M. DENT & SONS LTD
Aldine House, Albemarle Street, London

This book is set in 11 on 12 pt Garamond 156

ISBN 0 460 04183 5

Contents

List of Plates

List of Text-figures

List of Text-figures

Preface

Archaeology is nowadays taken to mean the study of objects which provide evidence of the activities and environment of the men of past centuries. Woodland and trees sometimes come within the archaeologist's province, because of their longevity and continuity and the many ways in which they interact with human affairs. In the case of some woodland the continuity of the plant community extends beyond the life-span of the individual trees.

As a rough rule I propose to exclude any tree or group of trees that has obviously been planted for some designed life-span that has not yet expired. A commercial orchard or forestry plantation acquires archaeological interest only if, for some reason, it is allowed to remain in existence beyond its commercial life-span and so to tell us about past, rather than current, practices. On similar grounds I shall seldom refer to the trees of gardens or town streets. Such exclusions leave us with woods that, in their present form, have not (or not obviously) been planted; with hedgerows; and with the trees of parks, meadows, commons, farmyards, and places like Epping Forest. These form the subject-matter of this book.

Except for gardens and forestry plantations, which have been charted by a number of competent historians but have relatively little archaeological interest, the literature on the history of trees and woods is very unsatisfactory. Some scholarly works have been written by foresters, whose interests are in plantations rather than in alternative and older methods of handling trees. Others have been written by historians who have worked among archives and are reluctant to put on their boots and discover what the land itself, and the things that grow on it, have to say.

At a more popular level, the subject has suffered from a long tradition of plagiarization and an unusually extensive corpus of folk-mythology; when they use contemporary evidence at all, many writers pay more attention to the exhortatory side of works like Evelyn's *Sylva* than to accounts of what actually happened in particular places.

The making of the [Norfolk] Broads by J. M. Lambert and others (1960) was a pioneer work in historical ecology, taking into account vegetation as a third dimension in a historical and archaeological synthesis. It is only in the case of hedges that this dimension has yet been constructed on anything like a national scale, but there are some half-dozen regional and local studies involving woodland and trees. Usually these are done by botanists, for they require a basic knowledge of the properties of indigenous trees and other plants which is seldom possessed by historians and not always by foresters. Such a historical outlook is to be found, for instance, in Mr Colin Tubbs's book on the New Forest, Dr Ruth Tittensor's study of the Loch Lomond oak woods, and Dr G. F. Peterken's work in Lincolnshire and Northamptonshire.

In the present state of knowledge it would be impossible to cover the British Isles uniformly without resorting to facile generalizations. As long ago as 1897 F. W. Maitland warned us in *Domesday Book and Beyond* that we ignore at our peril the intricate regional variation, so characteristic of Britain, of which much still remains despite all the levelling-out influences of the last 250 years. This book says more about the English lowlands than about highland regions, because of the nature of the subject; as far as we know it is chiefly in the lowlands that a stable relationship has developed between men and trees. The bias towards 'Eastern England'—Norfolk, Suffolk, Essex, and Cambridgeshire—results from my own research interests, which make it possible to tell a reasonably comprehensive story for this region and to point out how far other people's study areas differ. Eastern England is a particularly well-documented region which throughout historical times has had relatively little woodland though plenty of trees. It abounds in delicate variation and intricate detail. It has been less thoroughly swept by changes in silvicultural fashion than have many better-wooded areas, and is still rich in the fabric and traditions of medieval woodland.

In writing at this stage in the development of the subject I hope I may encourage readers to work on the many districts and counties that are still unexplored. Time is running out. The historical flow of change in the countryside—an erratic trickle with spates now and then—has turned since 1950 into a devouring flood from which little, at least in the eastern half of Britain, is safe. To plan rationally for the future we need to know about the origin and past maintenance of the details that we now prize. I hope that conservation-minded readers may be helped to identify features which are worth preserving or restoring, and to avoid wasting effort on sites where preservation is impossible, unreasonable, or not worth while. Even if they fail in their objects, if they do their work properly they will have the satisfaction of ensuring that the achievements of our past civilization have not been allowed to perish unrecorded.

I wish to thank Dr D. Chapman, Mr D. P. Dymond, Mrs A. Hart, Mr W. Liddell, Mr J. Hunter, Mr P. Nicholson, Dr C. Owen, Dr G. F. Peterken, Mr C. E. Ranson, and the late Mr J. Saltmarsh for allowing me to use their unpublished work. I am indebted also to Mrs J. Deacon, of Cambridge University Quaternary Data-bank, and to the owners and custodians of archives listed in the references. I have received valuable advice and comments from Dr D. E. Coombe, Mr Dymond, Mr W. H. Palmer, Dr Peterken, Professor C. D. Pigott, and Mrs R. Tittensor.

Plate xiv is from Cambridge University Collection (Committee for Aerial Photography), and Plates vii, xii and xiii are by Mr W. H. Palmer; copyright reserved. The quotation on page 39 is by permission of Danmarks Geologishe Undersøgelse.

I have made use of work done under a research grant from the Natural Environment Research Council to Cambridge University Botany School, in which I have been assisted by Mrs H. Heygate and Mrs S. Ranson.

My special thanks are due to Colin and Susan Ranson, whose encouragement and hospitality have enabled me to write this book. They have helped me in the field and the archives and have made many useful suggestions. Mrs Ranson typed the manuscript.

1 Introduction: how woods and trees work

Robert de Corneville was summoned [to explain] why he had committed waste contrary to the orders of our lord the king in a wood in Parva Tolleslund [Tolleshunt Knights, Essex] ... he felled the great oaks in the war and afterwards allowed his own cattle and oxen to eat the stool-shoots, so that he did waste and damage to the value of 60 shillings.

Curia Regis Rolls, A.D. 1220

Britain and its regions

For hundreds of years Britain has been one of the least wooded countries in Europe, but not all parts of Britain are equally poor in woodland, nor are they poorly wooded for the same reasons. Suffolk, at one extreme, has long been one of the least wooded counties, yet locally grown timber and wood have been very important to its inhabitants. At least a thousand years ago, men learned to live with their woods, to run them as a self-renewing resource, to derive their woodland products by intensive management of small wooded areas, and to devote the rest of the county to other uses. At the other extreme, most of Scotland until the eighteenth century was a comparatively thinly populated land, where trees were relatively unimportant because there were plenty of alternative resources of coal, peat, and building stone. Some ancient woodland survives, mainly by accident rather than design, in remote places; but the woods of the more populous parts of Scotland owe far more to later planting than to the medieval traditions of conservation and symbiosis which have shaped the Suffolk landscape.

Suffolk and Scotland are extreme examples of the two main types of woodland history in Britain. To a large extent these

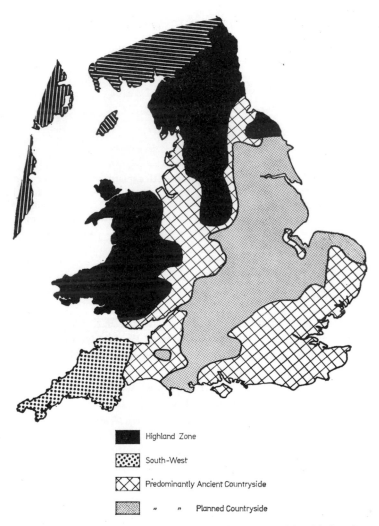

	Highland Zone
	South-West
	Predominantly Ancient Countryside
	" " Planned Countryside

Fig. 1. Regions of England and Wales, as used in this book.

correspond (Fig. 1) to the geographers' Highland and Lowland Zones. Wales, Ireland, and highland England appear to have tree histories not unlike Scotland; while the tradition of woodland as a form of intensive land use is repeated, not always to the same degree, in much of lowland England. Devon and Cornwall have lowland-type woodland histories but with some features (for example, the treatment of oak as coppice) more typical of highland practice.

A further distinction must be made. It used to be thought that the typical lowland countryside of hedged fields and small woods was derived from the 'enclosure movement' of the eighteenth and nineteenth centuries, before which nearly all England had been farmed in great open fields resembling, in some respects, the 'prairie farming' which is now becoming widespread in arable districts. Al hough in 1912 F. C. K. Gonner [1] exploded this myth by showing that parliamentary Enclosure Acts covered less than a fifth of England, it is even now widely repeated. At a reasonable estimate, allowing for enclosure by processes other than Act of Parliament and for areas still unenclosed, roughly half the hedged and walled landscape of England dates in fact from periods between the Bronze Age (Pollard and others 1974) and the seventeenth century. These enclosures are of very varied origins but have in common a characteristic irregularity resulting from centuries of casual 'do-it-yourself' enclosure and piecemeal alteration (frontispiece). This I shall call *Ancient Countryside*. In contrast, the *Planned Countryside* of post-1700 enclosure was usually laid out hurriedly on a drawing-board at the enclosure of each parish, and in consequence has a mass-produced quality of regular fields and straight roads.

This is one facet of a distinction that cuts deep in European social history. The Ancient Countryside, the *bocage*, is the land of hamlets, of medieval farms in hollows of the hills, of lonely moats in the clay-lands, of immense mileages of quiet minor roads, hollow-ways, and intricate footpaths; of irregularly shaped groves and thick hedges colourful with maple, dogwood, and spindle; and of pollards and other ancient trees. The Planned Countryside, the *champagne*, is the land of brick box-like farms in exposed positions, of thin hawthorn hedges, of ivy-laden clumps of trees in the corners of fields, of relatively few roads, and above all of straight lines, although it often contains medieval woods, Anglo-Saxon hedges, and ancient trees that the enclosure commissioners failed to destroy.

The distinction between the two types of landscape, though often very sharp, is too intricate to be mapped accurately on a

national scale. It is useful, however, to map (Fig. 1) those parts
of lowland England which are predominantly Ancient Countryside, and those that are mainly Planned.

Forestry, woodmanship, and wood-pasture

Trees are to be found on three types of site:

a) in *plantations*, where the trees are all of one age, often of one
kind, and have been deliberately planted;

b) in *woods*, where the trees are of different ages, or different
species, or both, and have not (or not all) been intentionally
planted;

c) in sites such as parks, hedges, and commons, where the growing of trees is subordinate to some other land use.

Although intermediates are common, especially in highland
areas, these types of tree-land correspond to three classes of
techniques for growing trees and to three traditions—I shall call
them *forestry*, *woodmanship*, and *wood-pasture*—which originated
independently and to a very large extent have gone their separate
ways down the centuries. Forestry (in the modern sense of the
word) is usually in Britain a matter of growing trees in plantations, like an arable crop. The ground is cleared and the trees
planted, grown, and finally harvested; the stumps are then
intended to die, and the ground is either replanted or put to
some other use. Woodmanship is the art of getting timber and
wood without destroying the existing vegetation; it uses the
facility that most British tree species have of growing again after
felling. Wood-pasture is the art of growing trees in the presence
of grazing animals. This book is about woodmanship and wood-
pasture, the history of which cannot be learned from forestry
books but has to be reconstructed from field and archaeological evidence and from the chance survival of workaday
documents.

Some kinds of tree, such as the ordinary 'pedunculate' oak,
occur equally on all three sorts of tree-land, while others are
more restricted. One seldom sees Sitka spruce outside plantations
or small-leaved lime except in a wood, while black poplar is very
strictly a non-woodland tree.

The biology of trees

There are many excellent textbooks on trees and their biology, but most of them are written by foresters or gardeners, who are interested in different kinds of trees, and in different aspects of their behaviour, from those which concerned our ancestors. There is a curious lack of knowledge and research about the biology of *native* trees, even such common species as elm and maple, and therefore I shall review some of their essential but less widely known ecological properties.

The botanists' distinction between *trees*, which have one main stem, and *shrubs*, which branch near or below ground level into several main stems, is not very useful to us because many trees, such as oak and ash, have often been grown in a multi-stemmed form. To save vain repetition the word 'tree' throughout this book will be taken to include large shrubs such as hazel.

Native, naturalized, and exotic trees

The British tree and shrub flora comprises between fifty and seventy *native* species, such as ash, hazel, and holly, which arrived here in prehistoric times. Some elms may have been imported by prehistoric men.

Three species are widely *naturalized*. Originally introduced from overseas, they now behave like native trees in that they maintain themselves indefinitely without human intervention and have widely invaded native vegetation. Sweet-chestnut was introduced in Roman times, sycamore in the Middle Ages, and *Rhododendron ponticum* more recently.

Several hundred kinds of tree are *exotic*, either imported from overseas at different times—connoisseurs of historical films will remember the anachronism of Sir Thomas More being executed against a background of horse-chestnuts!—or invented by gardeners, like London plane and some poplars. Exotic trees predominate in plantations and gardens, and a few, such as Sitka spruce and *Pinus pinaster*, are locally self-sown; but foreign species have not overrun the landscape at large to the extent that they have in some other countries. Even species like Norway spruce, which grow nearby on the Continent and were with us in earlier interglacials, are reluctant to reproduce their kind and seldom grow except where men have put them. This category includes all conifers except Scots pine, yew, and juniper, besides many broad-leaves.

Scots pine survives as a native tree only in the Scottish Highlands, while beech is native in certain districts south of a line from Carmarthen to King's Lynn. Both trees are widely planted and naturalized outside their native ranges.

How trees are replaced

Poets have accustomed us to the notion that trees, like the rest of us, reproduce their kind by sexual methods, in this case by acorns and other seeds. This is partly true but the matter is not simple. For instance, it is extremely easy to grow an oak tree from an acorn in one's garden, but it may be extremely difficult to do so in an existing wood. Some native trees such as small-leaved lime are almost never observed to establish themselves successfully from seed. The checks and balances of natural population control among trees are still little understood, but one important factor is that most British trees do not like shade. They will not grow up underneath bigger trees of the same species, but only in natural or artificial clearings, or sometimes under the lighter shade of other tree species. Beech, for instance, is shade-resistant and will grow slowly under oak; oak will grow up under birch; but birch demands light and will grow up only in the open.

Unless misused, native woods have a strikingly trouble-free record. Although woodland trees often reproduced by seed more freely in the past than they do now, woodmen made full use of other methods of regeneration by which a stand of trees could often be maintained indefinitely with little or no need for seedlings. Every gardener knows that some trees, such as pines, can be got rid of by cutting them down, but many species grow again from either the stump or the root system. Maple and wych-elm, for

Fig. 2. Different ways of managing wood-producing trees. For each method the tree, or group of trees, is shown just before cutting, just after cutting, and one year after cutting. All drawn to the same scale.

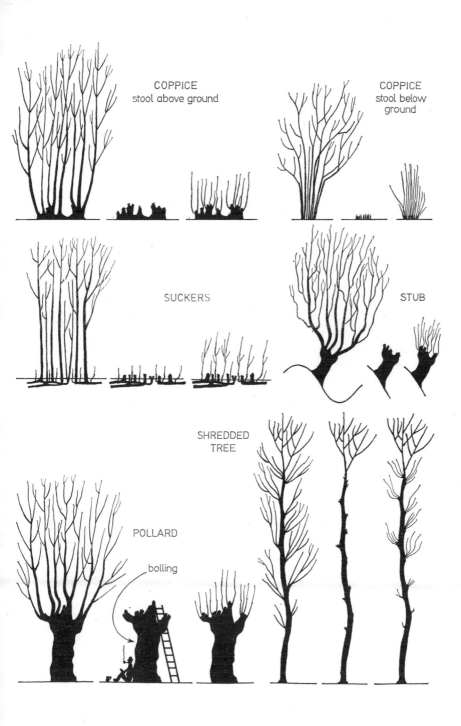

COPPICE
stool above ground

COPPICE
stool below
ground

SUCKERS

STUB

SHREDDED
TREE

POLLARD

bolling

instance, *coppice*; the stump sends up shoots and becomes a *stool*
from which an indefinite succession of crops of poles or *slop* can
be cut at intervals of years (Fig. 2). Aspen and most elms *sucker*;
the stump normally dies but the root system remains alive
indefinitely and sends up successive crops of poles, forming a
patch of genetically identical trees called a *clone*.

Coppicing and suckering are very efficient and reliable methods
of establishing a new crop. The rate of growth of poles varies
with species and site, but can exceed 2 inches *a day*; sallow
sometimes grows 11 feet high in the first summer after felling,
while even oak can stand 7 feet high and an inch thick after one
season's growth. Such shoots are largely immune from rabbits,
hares, and other destroyers of seedlings. But, as we see from the
quotation at the head of the chapter, they are greedily eaten by
cattle (and also by sheep and deer); and for this reason different
methods were adopted in wood-pasture and non-woodland
situations where these animals could not be fenced out. *Pollarding,
lopping,* or *cobbing* is the practice of cutting a tree at between
6 and 15 feet above the ground, leaving a permanent trunk called
a *bolling* (to rhyme with 'rolling'). This sprouts in the same way
as a coppice stool, but at a height where the animals cannot
reach the shoots, and yields an indefinite succession of crops of
poles. Pollarded trees survive mainly in south and east England,
especially Essex, and in the Lake District, but were formerly
more widespread. Before the modern bow-saw, pollarding was
disagreeable work—axes and ladders don't go well together!—
and coppicing was preferred where possible. All trees that coppice can also be pollarded, with a few exceptions (for instance,
hazel) and additions (for example, suckering kinds of elm).
A variant of pollarding is *shredding*, in which the side-branches of a
tree are repeatedly cut off, leaving a tuft at the top. I know of no
surviving shredded trees in Britain, but the practice seems
frequently to be referred to in medieval documents, and such
trees can still be seen in parts of France and Italy. Pollard trees
also serve to mark land boundaries, and for this purpose they are
sometimes cut not more than 4–6 feet high, forming *stubs*.

Timber and wood

In the days when woodmanship flourished it left its mark, like other crafts, on the English language. *Timber* and *wood* traditionally mean different things. Timber, medieval Latin *meremium*, is big stuff suitable for making planks, beams, and gate-posts; wood (Latin *boscus*) is poles, brushwood, and similar small stuff suitable for light construction or for firewood. The distinction has been important both in law and practice (for instance, tithes were payable on wood but not timber) and exact definitions, such as that wood is anything less than 2 feet in girth, have been laid down. Even now we talk of 'timber' buildings and 'wood' fires.

Wood consists either of *underwood* (Latin *subboscus*), the poles produced by cutting coppice, pollards, or young suckers, or of the branches of trees felled for timber. Timber trees, otherwise called *standards*, may be *maidens*, grown from seed or suckers, but have often originated by coppicing from the stumps of their predecessors. Typically a wood consists of timber trees and coppice stools; a park contains timber and pollards; while an ancient hedge contains coppice, suckers, pollards, and timber. The underwood, of course, is felled at more frequent intervals than the timber trees; underwood and timber in the same wood often belong to different people. Nowadays timber is much more highly valued than wood, but in the past wood has often been the more important crop, and it may yet be so again in the future.

The longevity of trees

Trees are long-lived creatures which are easily and permanently altered by their environment and by human activities. An ancient tree (Plate XIII) stores up information about what has gone on around it. Its very existence may tell us something of land use at the time when it originated. Its shape and branching and the scars of old injuries record the vicissitudes of centuries. When cut down its annual rings tell us how old it was and form a record of the good and bad seasons of its lifetime.

There is a lot of romantic guesswork and little hard information about how long trees live and how old particular individuals are. Foresters are concerned with trees in the first third, or at most the first half, of their biological life-span. Middle-aged and old trees are more difficult to understand—human life isn't long enough—and have no commercial interest. The grower of an oak for timber will regard it as 'mature' at 150 years; if it still stands at 200 years it may be getting 'over-mature'—attacked by wood-rotting fungi which destroy its timber value—even though if left alone it may have another 200 years of life before it.

For this reason, timber trees of more than 250 years' growth are not normally to be found in woods. Occasionally it happens that a wood passes through the hands of a succession of owners each of whom forgets to fell the oaks or values them for their beauty more than for their timber; Londoners will know the magnificent old oaks of Ken Wood in Highgate. Ancient timber trees are to be found mainly in parks and hedges, where they are more often valued for beauty or shade. Trees whose function is not timber—pollards and coppice stools—may live much longer than timber trees. The cutting process actually prolongs their life, and they go on doing their job of producing useful crops of poles despite old age or decay.

A tree does not have a predetermined life-span like that of mankind. Every year it is obliged to lay down a new annual ring of wood over its trunk and all its living branches, twigs, and roots. The material for the new wood is made by the leaves, and the amount of material available is determined by the size and spread of the tree's crown of branches and foliage. The vigour of a tree depends largely on the ratio between the size of its crown, which determines its annual 'income' of new wood, and the surface area of trunk, branches, etc., which forms the 'commit-ments' over which the new wood has to be spread. In its youth, the tree grows in height and its crown gets bigger each year. Eventually it reaches its maximum height and crown size and enters middle age. Its commitments inexorably rise, as its trunk, etc. get thicker; but its income remains fixed, apart from the effects of the weather of good and bad years and of room for expansion which may be created by the felling of neighbouring trees, both of which influences leave their record in wide or narrow annual rings. Old age begins when the tree can no longer meet its commitments and branches start to die.

The life-span of a tree is determined partly by the length of

Fig. 3.　Stag-headed tree.

time which it takes to reach old age and partly by the length of
time which old age lasts. The onset of old age is determined more
by the size of the tree than by the number of its years; a tree
that grows fast when young is likely to reach an early middle and
old age. When growth is slowed by an adverse environment or by
pruning or cutting, life is likely to be prolonged, as we see to an
extreme degree in the long lives of the bristle-cone pines of the
Arizona mountains. In the case of pollards and coppice stools,
the increase in the tree's commitments is interrupted each time it is
cut, and the ageing process begins from the date of the last cutting.

The power of a tree to prolong its old age depends on its
capacity for retrenchment and for recovering from damage, and
on the resistance of its heartwood to decay. Retrenchment is best
illustrated by the 'stag-headed' oaks of hedges and parks (Fig. 3),

whose dead upper branches show that they once had a larger active crown. Stag-head is widely misunderstood as a fatal condition; but in practice many stag-headed trees have been in that state for several decades—the bark and sapwood of the dead branches have rotted away—and the remaining crown is often in good health. Retrenchment and resistance to decay are best shown by non-woodland oaks and sweet-chestnuts, while elms often recover vigorously from severe damage. Beeches and ashes lack these qualities.

The recipe for longevity in an oak is that it should grow in a non-woodland site with plenty of room, on a poor soil; it should form a small crown; it should be a pollard or otherwise useless as timber; and it should have burrs and ridges on its trunk (genetically determined) which will enable it to form new branches late in life. Parkland oaks that combine all these qualities are astonishingly tenacious of life. All major branches may have been lost so long ago that even their heartwood has vanished; the tree may be reduced to the shell of a gigantic bolling; retrenchment may have gone so far that areas of bark have died and rotted away; yet strips of living tissue still cover burry ridges and maintain a small but healthy crown and a moss-like growth of short living twigs.

How old is a tree ?

Working out the age of a living tree is not an art that can be learned from books. The following are some of the factors involved.

The ultimate authority for the age of a tree is the number of annual rings when it is felled. Even if the tree is hollow, which most old trees are, one can often find a place where rotten but readable wood reaches nearly to the centre. In estimating how many rings have disappeared from a hollow tree, one must remember that trees usually grow faster when young. If possible one should cut a slice from the tree to examine in good conditions at home. Sometimes one can find an exposed section in a living tree, for example, in the stump of a sawn-off branch. Hollow borers for taking core samples seldom work well with big hardwood trees.

A useful rule, due to A. F. Mitchell (1974), is that a free-standing tree has 1 inch of girth (measured at 'breast height', 5 feet from the ground) for every year of its age; a tree in a wood has ½ inch of girth per year. These figures correspond to mean annual ring widths of 4.0 mm and 2.0 mm. This works very well for *maiden* trees of a variety of species in *middle age*. Most trees grow faster when young and slower when old. A few famous big oaks have been measured repeatedly over fifty to sixty years; on this basis Mitchell estimates that the Major Oak in Sherwood Forest, 402 inches in girth (10½ feet in diameter) in 1965, was then between 400 and 640 years old.[2]

Very large trees, however, are usually on good soil and are not necessarily the oldest. A moderately large tree with a small crown on a waterlogged or infertile site may be older than a well-favoured giant with a big crown. Pollards tend to be older than maidens of the same size: an actively pollarded tree has a very small crown, especially in the first few years after cutting, and hence the bolling expands very slowly. After pollarding has ceased it may form a full-sized crown and grow at much the same rate as a maiden. For an extreme example, I have found oak pollards in Epping Forest of only 50 inches girth which are at least 350 years old, having maintained an average ring width of 0.4 mm since 1720; this must be close to the slowest rate at which an oak can grow and yet remain alive. Oaks which are much retrenched in old age probably grow at about this rate.

An age of at least 400 years is quite often reached by oaks, especially pollards, in parks and Royal Forests. A few giants on poor sites go back much further, like the oak whose shattered bolling stands before the Dower House in Ickworth Park, W. Suffolk, and whose visible annual rings suggest an age of about 700. Other species rarely live beyond 500 years, except perhaps yew, which is long-lived by tradition but has seldom been scientifically dated. The pollard beeches of Burnham Beeches, Buckinghamshire, Epping Forest, and Felbrigg, Norfolk (Plate VIII), are known or suspected to be 300 to 400 years old. Ancient slow-grown beeches (and hollies) can sometimes be recognized by still-legible nineteenth-century graffiti (Fig. 4). Other pollarded trees—elm, ash, hornbeam, small-leaved lime—

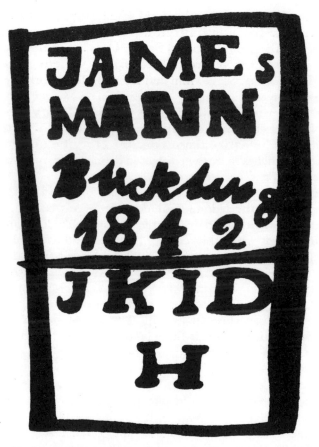

Fig. 4. Early graffito on a slowly-growing beech tree. The bark of beech and holly stretches as the trunk expands; the degree to which an inscription has been distorted gives a rough estimate of how much growth has occurred since it was cut. Genuine nineteenth-century graffiti have carefully executed lettering often (as here) in two different styles.

may live for about the same length of time, though pollard willows appear to be fast-growing and short-lived.

Longer-lived than maiden trees, or even pollards, are coppice stools. These are completely self-renewing and capable of living indefinitely as long as they are not directly overshadowed by timber trees. An old stool spreads, without loss of vigour, into a ring of living tissue with a decayed centre and often an interrupted circumference. Some species are cut on a high stool which can be sectioned to observe annual rings from which the rate of spread can be estimated. In the case of ash, on a waterlogged site a stool 2 feet across can be 300 years old (Rackham 1975), while on a good site a 300-year-old stool may be 5 feet across. Ancient stools are sometimes twice or even three times this diameter (Plate IX). The largest ash stool I have seen is in Felsham Hall Wood, W. Suffolk, 18½ feet across, on a rather wet site; it may be one of the oldest living things in Britain (at least a thousand years) but still yields a good crop of poles.

Small-leaved lime, elm, sweet-chestnut, beech, alder, and oak also form giant stools. Elm and sweet-chestnut grow faster than ash, but even so the imposing chestnut stools in Holbrook Park, E. Suffolk, up to 16 feet across, can hardly be later than the Middle Ages. Care should be taken not to confuse big single stools with the groups of stools formed by *layering*—bending down coppice poles and pegging them to the ground to take root—a method formerly used in some districts to propagate underwood.

What annual rings tell us

The annual rings of a middle-aged or old tree show seemingly random fluctuations which express the effects of weather or caterpillars year by year. These do not concern us directly, although they enable archaeologists to date oaken artifacts by recognizing particular runs of good and bad years. These yearly changes are superimposed on longer-term variations which reflect the general vigour of the tree. We can get a *release cycle* of wider rings (Fig. 5a) when a neighbouring tree dies and our tree expands to fill the gap. Conversely we can get a *damage cycle* of narrower rings (Fig. 5b) when our tree suffers some accidental loss of branches which are gradually replaced. A useful kind of damage cycle is seen in sections of bollings and of the bases of stools (Fig. 5c); it enables us to work out when, and at what intervals, the tree was pollarded or coppiced.

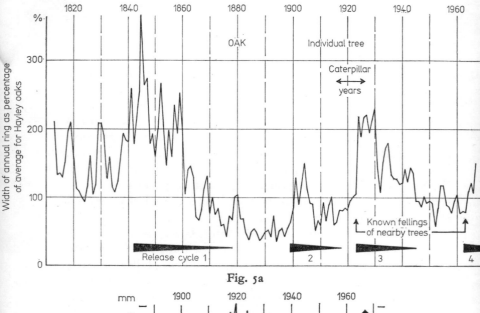

Fig. 5a

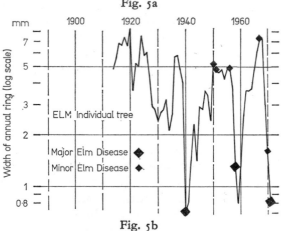

Fig. 5b

Fig. 5.   Tree-ring sequences.

a) A woodland oak, showing four periods of faster growth attributable to the felling of neighbouring trees. In this case ring-widths are expressed as percentages of the average ring-width for oak in each year in order to separate the release cycles of this particular tree from the effects of weather, etc., which are common to all oak trees. Hayley Wood, Cambridgeshire. b) A woodland elm, showing two cycles of slow growth following severe Dutch Elm Disease. A third major attack killed the tree. Hayley Wood. c) Bolling of a park pollard, showing seven cycles of sudden decline on pollarding followed by gradual recovery. Intervals between pollardings vary. Year-to-year fluctuations are superimposed on this pattern. Ipswich.

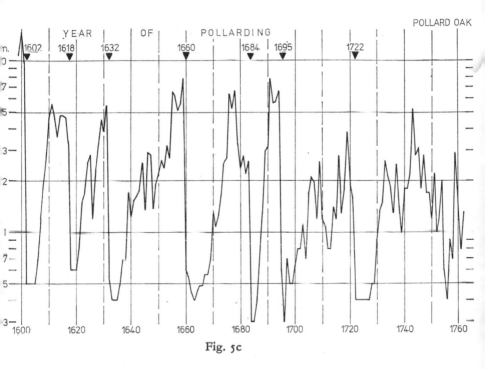

Fig. 5c

Woods of different kinds

To many botanists nearly every wood is an oak wood. It is
supposed that if Britain had been left alone by man the 'natural'
vegetation would nearly everywhere be oak-dominated forest.
On the strength of this hypothesis most woods, whatever their
actual composition, are interpreted as modifications of potential
oak wood. Only in places where oak is supposedly incapable of
growing are beechwood, pinewood, etc. recognized as plant
communities in their own right.

The theoretical basis of such a treatment is not as strong as it
was thought to be when, for instance, Sir Arthur Tansley wrote
his classic *British Islands and their Vegetation* (1939). The present
prominence of oak is not due everywhere to natural factors but
partly to the decision of past woodmen to treat it as timber rather
than underwood. By concentrating on oak woods botanists have
somewhat neglected the rich variety which native woodlands
actually present, particularly in their underwood. We have
maple woods, alder woods, hazel woods, lime woods, and several

31

sorts of elm wood. In eastern England alone, any one of at least fourteen native trees can predominate locally. Nearly every wood has its individual peculiarities. Often there is a mixture of up to a dozen trees and shrubs, and in many ancient woods the tree mixture varies in a complex way from one part of the wood to another. Wood-pastures, on the whole, are less variable, and contain fewer sorts of tree, than nearby coppice woods.

As yet this variation has not been completely mapped, let alone explained. Its origins lie partly in the historical influences of management and succession (for which see later in this chapter), and partly in the preferences which trees have in matters of soil and climate. We have often been misled as to what such preferences actually are, especially as the environments in which a particular tree is thought to produce good timber may not be the same as the range over which it is actually found growing. Beech is popularly supposed to be a tree of the chalk, although some of the best-known stands, for example, Burnham Beeches, are on very acid sands and gravels. In East Anglia some sorts of elm live happily on similar soils instead of the chalky clays which in theory elms prefer.

Primary and secondary woodland

Woodland and wood-pasture may have been formed from fragments of the prehistoric forest that have been brought under management without ever having been cleared of trees. In this case they will be termed *primary*. *Secondary* woodland and wood-pasture, in contrast, have been formed on areas that at some time in the historical period have been farmland, moorland, etc.

The natural tendency of almost any land in Britain is to turn into secondary woodland. Let a field be abandoned—as has happened to many fields down the centuries—and in ten years it will be overgrown and difficult to reclaim; in thirty years it will have 'tumbled down to woodland' or at least to scrub. The same would happen to most of our chalk downs, heaths, moorlands, and even mountains were it not prevented by grazing and burning.

The forester, no less than the farmer, is concerned to prevent his land from turning into natural woodland and to remove any native 'weed' trees that might compete with the crop. These efforts are not always successful and many plantations have come, through crop failure, neglect, or lack of replanting, to resemble spontaneous secondary woodland. The end-product is often self-sown birch wood with occasional residual conifers.

An abandoned field or plantation can be invaded by many species of tree, depending above all on what trees are growing near by which can seed or sucker into it. In the classic case—Broadbalk Wilderness at Rothamsted, Hertfordshire—an area of arable land was abandoned as an experiment in 1882 and within thirty-two years had become an oak-sycamore grove. Birch, elm, oak and hawthorn are probably the commonest early colonizers.

Successions

Succession is the spontaneous replacement of one type of vegetation by another, whether in an abandoned field or in an existing —even in a primary—wood. Ecologists traditionally believe that there is always a *climax* type of vegetation, oak-dominated forest in most of Britain, which will eventually prevail regardless of the colonization processes by which it is attained. This doctrine is perhaps true, but the climax may not be as simple as this, and the conditions for its fulfilment—several centuries of unchanging climate and freedom from human interference—are unrealistic. We sometimes see a secondary birch wood giving way to oak, but in ancient woods we just as often observe the reverse.

In the West Cambridgeshire woods for at least three hundred years the native ash, maple, and oak have been slowly and permanently squeezed out by elm (Rackham 1975). Sometimes succession results from a change of management: in Epping Forest a hundred years of abandoned pollarding have resulted in oak giving way to beech. Ash, sycamore, and occasionally even maple can also replace oak. The oak might hypothetically return in the long run, but in the long run woods are always complicated by management.

Summary of the properties of trees

Table 1 summarizes the behaviour of some of those trees which are of interest in the context of this book.

Table 1. Summary of the properties of the principal trees in this book

Older vernacular name	Botanical Latin name	Methods of Regeneration				Preference for woodland	Ability to form secondary woodland	Tolerance of poor soils
		Seed	Suckers	Coppicing	Pollarding			
NATIVE								
Alder —	Alnus glutinosa	+++	O	++++	?	−	+	++
Apple (crab) Wilding	Malus sylvestris	+++	O	+++	?	+	O	?
Ash —	Fraxinus excelsior	+++	O	++++	+++	O	++	+
Beech —	Fagus sylvatica	+++	O	++	+++	+	+++	+++
Birch (black) —	Betula pubescens	++++	O	++	?	O	+++	+++
(silver) —	B. verrucosa	++++	O	++	?	O	++	+++
Blackthorn —	Prunus spinosa	++	+++	O	O	−	++	+
Cherry (wild) Gean	P. avium	+++	+++	O	?	+	+	O
Elder —	Sambucus nigra	++++	O	(+++−)	?	O	++	O
Elm (wych) —	Ulmus glabra	++++	O	++++	++++	O	O?	+++
(smooth-leaved) —	U. carpinifolia (minor)	+	+++	(+)	+++	O	++	++
(English) —	U. procera	O?	++++	(+)	+++	−	+++	++
Hawthorn (hedgerow) Whitethorn, Quickthorn	Crataegus monogyna	++++	O	+++		O	++	++
(woodland) —	C. laevigata (oxyacanthoides)		O	+++	O?	+++	+++	++
Hazel Nuttery	Corylus avellana	++	O	++++	+	O	O	++
Holly Hulver	Ilex aquifolium	++	O	+++	+++	+	++	++++

Common name	Other name	Botanical name							
Hornbeam	Hardbeam	Carpinus betulus	+++	O	+++	+–+++	+–++	++	+++
Lime (small-leaved)	Linden	Tilia cordata	++	+	+++	+–+++	+++	+++	O	+++
Maple	—	Acer campestre	++	O	+++	+++	O	+++	+
Oak (pedunculate)	——	Quercus robur	++	O	+++	+(+++)	O	+++	+++
(sessile)	—	Q. petraea	++	O	+++	+(+++)	O	+++	+++
Pine (Scots)	—	Pinus sylvestris	+++	+–+	+++	+(+++)	O	+–+++	+++
Poplar (aspen)	Asp	Populus tremula	+	+	O	+++	O	+	+++
(black)	Popeler	P. nigra	O	+	O?	(+++)	O?	—	O?
(white)	Abele	P. alba	O?	+++	O	(+++)	O	—	+++
Rowan	Quicken	Sorbus aucuparia	+++	O	+++	?	+++	O	+++
Sallow	—	Salix caprea	+++	O	+++	(+++)	+++	O	+++
Sallow	—	S. cinerea (atrocinerea)	+++		++	+++	+++	O	+–+++
Service	—	Sorbus torminalis	++	O	+	O?	+	O	+–O
Whitebeam	—	S. aria	+	+–+	+–	?	+–+	++	+–O
Willow (crack)	—	Salix fragilis	+++	O	(+++)–+	O?	+–	—	+–O
(white)	—	S. alba	++	O	(+++)–+	O?	+–	—	O

NATURALIZED

Common name		Botanical name							
Chestnut (sweet)	—	Castanea sativa	++	O	+++(++++)?	++	O?	+++
Rhododendron	—	Rhododendron ponticum	++++	O	(++++)	O?	O	+++	+++
Sycamore	—	Acer pseudoplatanus	++++	O	+++(++++)	—	O	+++	+++

For explanation of symbols see page 36

Under 'Methods of Regeneration' the number of +'s in each column indicates roughly how easy it is for the tree to regenerate by the method in question. One + means that the method very rarely occurs; O means that I know of no *practical* instance of its operation. Brackets mean that the ability exists but has seldom been used in management.

'Preference for woodland' ranges from +++ (trees almost exclusively in woods) to — — — (hardly ever in woods). 'Ability to form secondary woodland' ranges from +++ (readily acts as a first colonizer) to + (late colonizer or weak first colonizer) and O (seldom or never occurs in secondary woodland). 'Tolerance of poor soils' ranges from ++++ to O.

Elms

Elms, especially in woods, are exceedingly complicated and only a very superficial account can be given. The wych-elm, the common elm of the north and west, is a 'normal' species, reasonably well defined and coming true from seed. It is not gregarious as are other elms. The 'English' elm, *Ulmus procera*, is the common elm of the Midlands, southern England, the Welsh Border, and South Essex, a massive, very erect tree that often stays green into December, nowadays the chief victim of Dutch Elm Disease; it comes from suckers rather than seed, but is not very variable. *Ulmus carpinifolia* is a collective name for the innumerable local sorts of elm in East Anglia, the East Midlands, and Cornwall, with their remarkable variation in leaf and bark and in their graceful or rugged manner of growth. New kinds arise through occasional hybridization and some are thought to have been imported in the past. Once established they maintain themselves automatically by suckering. Other groups of elms include *Ulmus stricta*, a name which covers the 'Cornish' elm and the Wheatley and Jersey elms of gardeners; the unnamed coppicing elms of some eastern woods; and hybrids between *glabra*, *procera*, and *carpinifolia* elms. Different sorts, especially among *carpinifolia* elms, vary greatly in their ecological behaviour and in the extent to which they invade woodland and hedges at the expense of the former trees. Elms were valued by our ancestors not only for timber and wood but also for shade, for hedging, and as an emergency food for beast and possibly even for man.

Limes

The familiar 'common' lime, *Tilia vulgaris*, planted in millions in towns and villages, is a hybrid between the 'large-leaved' lime, *T. platyphyllos*, and the 'small-leaved' lime, *T. cordata*. It became fashionable in the seventeenth century and is valued by nurserymen because easily propagated from suckers, but is rarely naturalized. Both *cordata* and *platyphyllos* are now known to be native to Britain. The small-leaved lime, a large and beautiful tree with its graceful bluish heart-shaped leaves, is of great historical interest (page 41 ff.). The large-leaved lime is a much rarer tree apparently confined to certain limestone areas. Natural hybrids occur, sometimes in woods with *cordata* but no pure *platyphyllos*.

Poplars

Of the innumerable poplars in Britain only four sorts are native or naturalized; they are nowadays less familiar than the exotic or artificial kinds such as Lombardy and Black Italian.

The aspen, a woodland poplar often referred to in medieval documents, presents no problem.

The black poplar is one of the rarest and most distinctive native trees; although recognizable a mile off by its outline (Fig. 6), it has been much confused with other poplars. Its trunk, which usually leans, is often 100 feet high and 6 feet thick, and has large rounded bosses in the lower part. The heavy branches always grow in arching curves. The bark is more rugged than in any other British tree. It grows generally in riverside meadows, never in woods. The word 'poplar' in pre-1650 documents, which refers to a very large non-woodland tree, appears to mean this species alone. In the Middle Ages it was one of the commonest trees in Suffolk and Essex. It can still be seen there, although E. Milne-Redhead tells me that there are estimated to be less than a thousand genuine black poplars left in Britain.

37

Fig. 6. Genuine black poplar, *Populus nigra*.

The white poplar is commonly supposed to have been introduced from Holland, along with its name *abele*, in the seventeenth
century. The word *abel*, however, occurs in a number of Suffolk
documents of the thirteenth and fourteenth centuries—the Rev.
J. T. Munday first pointed it out to me in the court rolls for
Brandon—as the name of a large tree sometimes referred to as a
different species from the *popeler*. This implies that the white
poplar is either native or anciently introduced.[3]

The grey poplar is now known to be a hybrid between white
poplar and aspen. It is sometimes naturalized; its origins and
ecology would repay investigation.

2 The Wildwood: prehistoric beginnings

The dominance of lime in the Post-Glacial warm period has only lately been realized. Examinations of peat-bogs can easily give an exaggerated impression of the significance of oak. . . . Lime flowers are pollinated by insects and thus do not disperse the pollen so effectively as the other common forest trees, which have flowers specialized for wind-pollination. . . . Lime was much more frequent and oak was much more scarce than the pollen diagrams would appear to suggest.

J. Iversen, *Danmarks Natur* (1967), trans. by Michael Robson

The history of woodland and trees in Britain begins about 8000 B.C. There have, of course, been trees of various sorts in the land for hundreds of millions of years, but these are not directly relevant to our purpose because the ecological continuity of our vegetation has been broken by the ice ages. Our story begins at the end of the last glaciation, when the return of a hospitable climate enabled some of the trees and other plants and animals that had retreated to more southerly latitudes to return to Britain.

Before written records, all the evidence for the history of trees has to come from actual remains, especially from pollen. Many plants, especially trees, produce large quantities of pollen grains which are extremely resistant to decay and which accumulate in stratified deposits such as peats and lake muds and also, though in a manner more difficult to interpret, in acid soils on dry land. Individual grains can be recognized to some extent under the microscope as coming from particular kinds of plant. For instance, it is easy to tell lime pollen from oak; the two species of lime can be separated with difficulty; but as far as we know it is impossible to tell apart the pollens of the two native oaks, of different poplars, or to separate willow from sallow.

For most of the post-glacial period the predominant vegetation of Britain has been continuous forest of various kinds. For brevity, and to avoid adding further to the meanings of the overworked word 'forest', I shall call these prehistoric forests by the general name of *Wildwood*. The rest of this chapter is an up-to-date summary of the relevant aspects of the many years of research which have been done on the British Wildwood. The standard work on it is Godwin (1975) and a shorter account is in Pennington (1969).

The development of the Wildwood

After one or more false starts, the post-glacial warm period, which we now enjoy, began quite rapidly around 8200 B.C. (I use the radiocarbon chronology). At that time Britain was largely treeless, but there was dry land across both the English Channel and the Irish Sea, and trees and other plants could move in from the Continent when the climate became suitable. A series of waves of colonization by different trees moved rapidly across the country from the south-east; there was of course no agricultural land to stand in the way of such invasion. The earliest Wildwood was formed by birch, that most arctic of trees, whose pollen, in the deposits, rapidly replaces that of the grasses and other non-woodland plants that had preceded it. About 7500 B.C. there was a similar expansion of pine, which quickly replaced most of the birch. Pine was followed in order by hazel, elm, oak, and alder. All these spread throughout Britain, except the far north of Scotland; alder got to Ireland shortly before it was cut off by rising sea-level. The next invader, lime, scarcely penetrated beyond the Lowland Zone of England.

The arrival of lime began a long period of relative stability—roughly 5500–3000 B.C.—during which the various tree species fought one another by the natural processes of succession to form a series of 'climax' forest types. At the end of this Atlantic Period, readily recognized in pollen profiles by a sudden fall in the abundance of elm, almost the whole of Britain was covered with virgin forest which was just beginning to be affected by human activities.

The fully developed Wildwood

A picture of the Wildwood just before the Elm Decline has been compiled by Dr John Birks and his colleagues (1975). It is derived from 140-odd pollen profiles from all over the British Isles, though there is a large blank area in midland and southern England where there are few suitable deposits.

The 'dry-land' tree assemblages of Birks's compilation fall into four regional types (Fig. 7). (We discount alder because it tends always to grow in the wet places where deposits form.) The Scottish Highlands, and small areas in the mountains of Ireland and the Lake District, were dominated by birch and pine. Hazel and elm dominated most of the rest of Ireland—and, on the slight available evidence, perhaps Cornwall and south-west Wales. Most of the remaining Highland Zone was dominated by oak and hazel. In the Lowland Zone, to summarize a complex situation, the commonest tree (for reasons explained at the head of the chapter) was almost certainly lime. This was combined with oak, hazel, and various other trees such as pine in the East Anglian Breckland and ash in Somerset.

These regional types, especially that of the Lowland Zone, each covered a patchwork of local forest variants, like those which still exist in the surviving Wildwood of remote parts of the world. Even within the birch-pine dominated region, Dr Hilary Birks [4] has shown that the patchwork of pine woods and oak woods, which still exists around Loch Maree, dates from 7000 B.C.

Even in 3000 B.C. we see the emergence of some features which persist in ancient woodlands to this day. The birch-pine forests of Scotland still remain in the form of the Highland pine woods and perhaps birch woods, though the Irish and English pines seem to be extinct. The hazel-elm Wildwood of Ireland may survive in the hazel woods of the Burren in County Clare. And the contrast between Highland and Lowland Zones, the former dominated by oak, the latter a mosaic of forest types in which lime was probably the commonest tree, still corresponds to a fundamental distinction of plant communities. A common and characteristic woodland type in the Highland Zone is oak coppice-with-standards, in which oak is dominant to such an

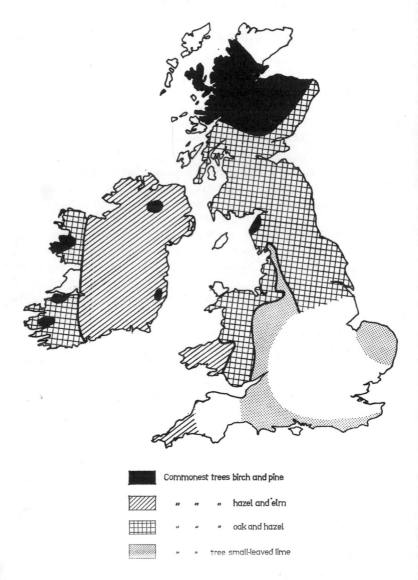

	Commonest trees birch and pine
	" " " hazel and elm
	" " " oak and hazel
	" " tree small-leaved lime

Fig. 7. Regional variation in the Wildwood just before the Elm Decline (about 3000 radiocarbon years B.C.). Derived from Birks and others (1975). No information exists for blank areas.

extent that it has been treated in recent centuries as underwood as well as timber. Only in a few widely scattered sites in the Lowland Zone is oak sufficiently abundant to have been coppiced; elsewhere it has been reserved and encouraged as a timber tree, while other species have been treated as underwood. In terms of their underwood, lowland woods (especially those of the east) are still a patchwork of communities: different woods, and different parts of the same wood, are composed of different mixtures of trees.

Native lime is now much less common than it was in 3000 B.C., but is an unobtrusive tree and is not as rare as is commonly supposed. Lime woods are still to be found, if one looks for them, over much of the prehistoric range of the tree. Fig. 8 illustrates a group of lime woods, almost unsuspected until 1969, in S. Suffolk, where lime grows in almost every ancient wood within a definite area (Plate 1). These, and similar groups of lime woods in Essex, Norfolk, Lincolnshire, Derbyshire, etc., are almost certainly the fragmented remains of parts of the Wildwood that were particularly rich in *Tilia*. Of the two species of lime, *T. platyphyllos* has always been much rarer than *T. cordata*, as is still the case.

In the absence of suitable pollen deposits, we can only speculate on how far the ash and maple woods of the Midlands, the beech woods of the Chilterns, and the hornbeam woods of Essex and Suffolk reflect vegetation differences already established before the Elm Decline, and how far they result from later changes. Ash was established, at least locally, in the Atlantic Period, but did not invade the Highland Zone in strength until later. Many, at least, of the northern ash woods are secondary woodland established after forest clearance in Neolithic times or, in some cases (Merton 1970), in very recent centuries. Holly appears to have a similar history. Beech got into Dorset in the Atlantic Period but along the south coast remained a rare tree until it, too, increased in abundance following human activity.

We still do not know much of what the Wildwood looked like, of its structure, how it reproduced, and what lived in it. Analogies with supposedly primeval forest in other temperate countries suggest that it contained many very old and large trees, with little underwood, and large quantities of rotten trunks lying on

43

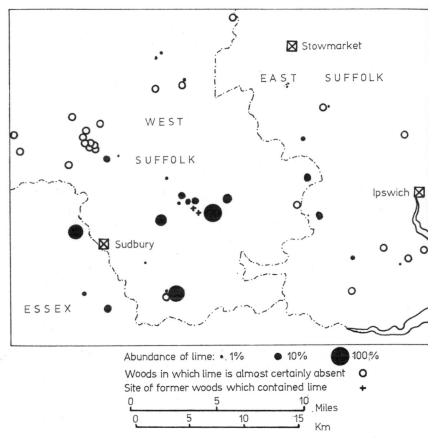

Abundance of lime: •.1%   ● 10%   ⬤ 100%
Woods in which lime is almost certainly absent O
Site of former woods which contained lime +

```
0          5          10
                         Miles
0      5      10      15
                         Km
```

Fig. 8. The Suffolk lime woods. Woods of less than 5 acres or of recent origin are ignored. Mostly from personal observation.

the ground or leaning against trees. These analogies may not be very sound since they do not allow for differences in the proportion of conifers or in the rate at which logs decay. The general frequency of hazel, which does not flower well in shade, suggests that in many places the big trees were patchy or scattered, allowing light to penetrate to the underwood. Trees presumably reproduced mainly by seed, but we know little of the conditions in which seedlings might become established. Did big trees rot at the roots and come crashing down to leave glades in which their successors could get started? Did they rot standing and fall to pieces gradually, leaving only a small gap? Or did the Wildwood consist of patches of trees all germinating, growing, maturing, and dying together?

Most woodland herbs and undershrubs are poorly recorded because they produce very little pollen. We know that brambles, dog's-mercury, bluebells, wood anemone, etc. go back to prehistoric times, and suspect that they increased in abundance as a result of human interference with the Wildwood. More or less permanent glades are suggested by the constant presence of grass pollen as well as by occasional grains of light-demanding herbs, such as willow-herbs and devil's-bit, which still grow on woodland rides. Such glades presumably provided grazing for deer and wild oxen which ate any tree saplings that appeared among the herbage.

We can actually touch the Wildwood in the 'buried forests', the stumps or logs preserved in peat in various places. In the Fens, for instance, there are the buried trunks of enormous 'bog oaks' and pines—lengths of 70 feet to the first branch have been reported—as well as willow, yew, and other trees. Part of this forest must have consisted of tall trees closely spaced; but in other places the trees are smaller, and we have no means of telling how far the forest of the Fens was representative of the Wildwood as a whole.

The destruction of the Wildwood

Human interference with the Wildwood perhaps goes back to the earliest post-glacial. Mesolithic men, though few in numbers and not tilling the soil, undoubtedly made small temporary clearings; they may also have set fire to whatever was combustible in the Wildwood, in order to drive out the game, and thereby have had a hand in such changes as the decline of pine in England.[5]

These controversial and doubtfully relevant matters apart, the earliest evidence of large-scale interference comes with the Elm Decline, which is remarkably sudden and remarkably synchronous at 3100–2900 B.C. The decline of elm is everywhere asscociated with a sudden increase in farm weeds such as plantains and stinging-nettle, and often—both in Great Britain and Ireland

—with archaeological evidence of early Neolithic settlement. There is now little doubt that it had something to do with the introduction of agriculture. In a land where as yet there was little grass, cattle may have been fed on leafy shoots shredded or pollarded from trees, especially elm, on a short cutting cycle which prevented trees so treated from flowering and producing pollen.

The destruction of the Wildwood for cultivation begins just after the Elm Decline and continues throughout the Neolithic and Bronze Ages and beyond. On the light soils of the East Anglian Breckland, where there was a dense, and even an industrial, Neolithic population, the Wildwood soon vanished never to return. The same probably happened on much of the chalk-lands and is recorded for the coastal fringe of the Lake District. Elsewhere clearances throughout the Neolithic were temporary; the pollen record suggests a scene rather like what one can still see in South Tirol, where grazing, cultivation, shredding, coppicing, and scrub co-exist uneasily side by side.

During the Bronze Age (1700–500 B.C.) clearance of the Wildwood continued and extended into high altitudes. Late in this period the climate became wetter and blanket bogs began to grow at the expense of the remaining forest. There is much dispute—irrelevant to this book—about the part played by climatic change and human activity in the development of moorland.

At various times in the late Neolithic and Bronze Ages the frequency of lime declines in many places. This decline is attributable to the deliberate grubbing out of lime woods—presumably because they were on the more fertile soils—leaving other types of Wildwood to be dealt with later.[6]

Around 400 B.C. the Celtic people entered Britain, bringing iron tools and heavy ploughs capable of tilling clay soils. The ensuing further expansion of agriculture takes us to the point at which the next chapter resumes the story.

To convert millions of acres of prehistoric forest into farmland is unquestionably the greatest achievement of our ancestors, who had a much smaller population than ours and no power tools. We know little of how they did it, of what men were involved, how they were organized, how much of their time they devoted to this activity, how many man-hours it took to clear an acre, or what they lived on while doing it. We are obliged to fall back on speculation, guided by analogy with various types of modern forest destruction and with experiments on simulating ancient methods of winning land and growing crops.7

The nature of the task must have varied enormously. Some conifer forests can be destroyed more or less permanently merely by setting fire to them; rhododendron scrub can only be cleared by digging up every bush. Most of the prehistoric forest of Britain must have come at various points between these extremes.

Our ancestors did not have enough chemistry or horsepower to poison or uproot unwanted woods as do the modern farmer and forester. Their main tools were axe, fire, and browsing animals. Compared with the world's trees as a whole, most native British species are difficult to burn, are not readily killed by felling because they coppice or sucker, but are eaten when young by cattle and sheep.

Apart from pine, which can be burnt standing, the most economical way of dealing with a forest that did not contain too many big trees would be by some combination of felling, burning, and browsing. I have not myself used a stone axe, but it is said to be as good as a metal one for cutting down smallish trees—some reports of experiments lead one to believe that it must compare favourably with a chain-saw! The regrowth problem could be reduced by burning up the felled trees on top of as many of the stumps as possible. Trees too big to fell could be killed by lighting fires round them or, less reliably, by ring-barking. The stumps and bigger logs would have to be ploughed around, as in nineteenth-century North America, for many years.

Cattle, sheep, and goats probably helped the axe clearance process by browsing the young regrowth shoots and eventually killing the stumps. Farm animals too were probably allowed to roam the remaining Wildwood and to scratch a living from such herbage as it contained. They would naturally eat tree seedlings as well and this could, in theory, result eventually in forest clearance: the dense Wildwood would change into parkland, as old trees died without being succeeded by young ones, and eventually into treeless grassland. This process tended to happen in medieval wood-pasture (page 135); but we should not exaggerate its importance. It takes rather a lot of browsing to stop regeneration altogether. Places like the unenclosed New Forest and Hatfield Forest have been heavily grazed for centuries and still have plenty of trees. C. R. Tubbs's New Forest studies (1968) suggest that regeneration has gone on whenever there has been less than about one bullock to four acres, or the equivalent in other animals; this is a surprisingly high density of stocking and we may doubt whether it often occurred in prehistoric times except very close to settlements.

Prehistoric woodmanship

The builders of henge monuments made light, when the spirit moved them, of finding and handling the huge timbers needed to make woodhenges. Our most detailed knowledge of how pre-historic peoples used timber and wood for more mundane purposes comes from the corduroy roads that they built across peat bogs.

Many Neolithic and Bronze Age trackways have been found in the Somerset Levels. They were built by a variety of methods from materials such as birch brushwood, ash and alder poles of various sizes, and oak logs. Most of them contain large quantities of straight poles of more or less uniform size, which are clearly not branches of trees, nor do they come from casual scrub. It is very unlikely that such poles could have been *found* in the Wild-wood; they must have been *grown* in managed woodland. In all probability they were produced by coppicing, though this has yet to be adequately confirmed by tree-ring analysis. The most sophisticated trackway, both in carpentry and woodmanship, is also the earliest (Coles and others 1973). It involves wood of oak, ash, lime, hazel, alder, and holly, of different sizes and selected for particular functions in the structure. The sizes and shapes of the assemblage of poles are remarkably like those produced by a medieval mixed coppice on a rather long rotation. An exact replica could easily be built out of the Bradfield Woods (page 80). The trackway is contemporary with the Elm Decline; with a date of 3174 radiocarbon years B.C., corresponding probably to 4000 actual years B.C., it seems to provide by far the earliest evidence of woodmanship in the world.

3 The Dark Ages of woodland: from Claudius to Hugo de Northwold

Start from Twyford along the road to Bracken Ridge, from there along the road to Carrion Barrow; then in a straight line to the pear tree; then along the road to Ceardic's Barrow; then to Withy Grove; then to the road that shoots over the ditch; then along the road to the pollard oak; from there along the road from where it adjoins the wood , , , by the little hedge along the spinney . . . along the hedge to the old maple tree . . . from there to the hoar [i.e. lichen-covered] apple tree; then along the ditch out to the River Test; to its southern bank; then along the bank; then below the timber weir to the northern bank; along the bank back to Twyford.

Boundary of Hurstbourne Priors (Hants), dated A.D. 901

The first twelve centuries after the birth of Christ are undoubtedly the most important period in the formation of the British countryside. In the year o the inroads of civilization on the wilderness, though rapidly advancing, were still comparatively local. By A.D. 1200 much of the modern landscape was already recognizable: nearly all our villages and most hamlets existed then, and the proportions of farmland, moorland, and woodland were not enormously different from what they are now. Most of the things that distinguish woodland from Wildwood—the separation of woods from each other, the naming of woods, their private ownership and defined boundaries, and above all *management* by rotational felling to provide a succession of crops and by fencing to protect the young growth from grazing animals— became widespread and systematic at some time during this period. Our modern woods are the tattered and patched, but still unmistakeable, remains of a fabric that was woven in this remote age.

We cannot claim to have much direct evidence of what was going on in these formative centuries. Pollen deposits—where

49

they exist and have not lost their upper layers through peat-digging or erosion—become progressively more uncertain of interpretation as the area from which they collect pollen develops into a patchwork of land uses. As woodland plays a decreasing part, it becomes difficult to sort out what is happening to the remaining woodland. We are too early for adequate written records. The classical authors tell us little of value, and neither the vivid glimpses of the countryside that we get from the Anglo-Saxon charters nor the enigmatic statistics of Domesday Book contribute to a continuous stream of documentation for particular sites. A promising source of evidence lies in the large quantities of timber that are nowadays being recovered from the excavation of waterlogged sites, which should, in principle, be capable of telling us about the structure and management of Roman and Anglo-Saxon woods. Until this material has been exploited we are forced to rely largely on the circumstantial, and often speculative, evidence that conventional archaeology gives of the extent of tree-land in Roman and Anglo-Saxon times and of the inhabitants' attitude towards it.

The first four centuries

When the Romans conquered England they found a land with a well-developed, if localized, agriculture. The Wildwood had vanished for ever from most of the lighter land such as river gravels and chalk-land. The introduction of the furrow-turning plough had made it possible to begin cultivating the clay-lands.

The Romans developed England and Wales into one of the chief agricultural and corn-exporting lands of the classical world. Although as yet the pollen evidence is largely confined to remote upland areas,[8] recent archaeological surveys have shown that this agricultural expansion extended throughout the lowlands: not only over the light soils around the great villas, but also into the difficult terrain of the Fens, the heavy clay-lands of Suffolk and Essex, and even into what were later to be heavily wooded areas such as Rockingham Forest, Northamptonshire, and Wychwood Forest, Oxfordshire. Only locally, as on the boulder-clay of East and West Cambridgeshire, were there (on present evidence) tracts of uninvaded Wildwood.

Roman Britain was also an industrial land in which timber and wood were the main structural materials for civil and military building and the main fuel for working iron and other metals and for making pottery, bricks, and salt. The notion that the Wildwood was always at hand to supply these needs and to be converted to farmland in the process is somewhat impractical. Apart from transport problems, the Romans were no better equipped than their medieval successors for chopping up into usable sizes the great trees which much of the Wildwood, particularly where it had been grazed, would have contained. It is much more plausible that wood supply and forest clearance were largely independent, and that as in later centuries areas of woodland were managed for the purpose of growing small and medium-sized trees. An isolated kiln or furnace might conceivably have worked on a temporary supply from a few suitable trees in the Wildwood, but a large-scale industry continuing for centuries clearly did not use up its fuel. Some kind of permanent coppice system must have stood behind the ironworks of the Weald and the Forest of Dean, the potteries of Castor (Peterborough) and Wattisfield (Suffolk), the bricks, tiles, and timber buildings of every Roman city, the wattle-and-daub of rural buildings, and (on a smaller scale) behind most bath-houses and hypocausts in forts and villas and behind every grain-drier on a farm.

The mixture of tree species identified from charcoal suggests that Roman woods looked not unlike the mixed coppices of post-medieval East Anglia.[9]

The coming of the Anglo-Saxons

How much of this survived the coming of the Anglo-Saxons? We used to regard the post-Roman scene as one of total dereliction —secondary woodland springing up over abandoned villas, roads and fields—out of which the invaders laboriously carved their own independent landscape. Nowadays archaeologists are coming round to the view, discussed for instance by C. C. Taylor[10] and by F. Emery,[11] that there was an overlap between the Roman and Anglo-Saxon cultures and that not only the main roads but a considerable amount of detail in our landscape are really of Romano-British origin. The ecological evidence, such as it is, favours this hypothesis. Some Roman settlements on the less profitable farmland became covered by woodland which occasionally has remained as such until now; but we find no hint of the massive return of secondary forest, invading even the good arable land, which we would expect to follow severe depopulation. Even the pollen diagram for Old Buckenham, Norfolk (Godwin, 1968), in the front line of the English invasion, suggests at most that forest clearance stopped for a while.

Although industrial uses of woodland declined, we must not suppose that management lapsed altogether. Men could no longer afford bricks and glass, and worked less in iron and copper, but they still cooked and warmed themselves, made pots and built houses. It is just possible that some of the oldest coppices in counties with strong Roman connections, such as Suffolk and Essex, might go back as managed woodland to the Romans.

However much farmland the Anglo-Saxons may have inherited, they eventually came to occupy nearly all the area settled in Roman times and to penetrate whatever Wildwood the Romans had left uninhabited. Several pollen diagrams show that there was a parallel phase of forest clearance by their contemporaries in the Lake District, Scotland, and Ireland. Some of this appears to date from the Roman–Anglo-Saxon overlap; one wonders whether refugees from the invasion were being forced to colonize the hills. For instance, at Bloak Moss, Ayrshire, Dr Judith Turner[12] has found extensive clearance, dated to the fifth or sixth century, which she has been able to show to involve not a general thinning of the forest but the creation of defined clearings within it.

Anglo-Saxon woodmanship

The Anglo-Saxons were carpenters rather than masons. Despite their long experience with stone they preferred to build in timber, except for churches, right up to the Conquest. We know of the technology only from tantalizing excavated remains and obscure literary references; from the church door at Hadstock, Essex, still in daily use after nearly a thousand years; and—if indeed it is Anglo-Saxon—from the mysterious church at Greensted, Essex, with its clever design and skilled workmanship.

The Anglo-Saxons did not go in for the 'log-cabin' buildings of the Continent, a building system that demands straight conifer poles which did not grow here. The British tradition, which began in prehistoric times and continued in various forms right into the twentieth century, is of timber-framed buildings with upright posts separated by panels which are filled with wattle-and-daub. This is a hardwood carpentry which depends on a supply of poles of various sizes, some of them very small, which need be only moderately straight. Such poles would normally have had to be grown in coppice woods.

Early Anglo-Saxon buildings had posts set in the ground; such structures would soon have rotted and their frequent replacement would have made proportionately heavy demands on timber supplies. The invention of the groundsill, a horizontal sleeper-beam into which the feet of the posts are morticed and which acts, among other things, as a damp-course, came in very gradually towards the latter part of the period.

The surviving scraps of early literary evidence include tariffs of compensation for criminal damage which show that trees could be valuable private property. King Ine of sixth-century Kent, for instance, decreed that a smallish tree, under which thirty swine could stand, was to be valued at 60 shillings (in Anglo-Saxon England one could get away with murder for 200 shillings). In South Wales a mere hazel stool was equivalent to 3¾ sheep.

Anglo-Saxon charters

These documents [13] give us our earliest chance to escape from treacherous generalities on to the firmer ground of describing some identifiable piece of country. It was customary, in the days before maps, for a deed of gift or sale of a piece of land to contain a *perambulation*, or description of the boundaries. The example at the head of the chapter shows how this was done. By careful field-work it is often possible to identify exactly the sites mentioned.

Reading these perambulations one is struck by how little England has changed in the thousand or so years since they were written. Nearly all the landmarks are of kinds that are still familiar to us: woods, hedges, streams, roads, ditches, rocks,

Table 2.   Single trees or groups mentioned in Anglo-Saxon perambulations

	50 charters mainly in S. England	100 charters in Worcestershire (after G. B. Grundy [14] and M. Hadfield)
Thorn (presumably mostly hawthorn)	23	23
Oak (including one 'saint's oak' and one pollard)	3	20
Apple	4	7
Sallow, willow, withy	5	4
Pear	3	4
Elder	5	0
Maple	3	2
Lime	0	5
Ash	2	2
Birch	0	3
Aspen	0	1
Holly	0	1
Service	0	1
Unspecified	10	—

and especially trees. The charters give our earliest evidence for hedges—often in terms such as 'thorn row' which make it quite clear that a hedge and not a fence is meant—and individual woods. For instance, the Ailsworth, Peterborough, charter in 948 refers to Moore Wood, which existed until the 1960s. Occasional references to pollard trees (for example, *coppedan ac*) are the earliest written allusion to this practice. Although they are not a random sample of the countryside (for example, most of them are south of the Thames) we can cautiously say that the charters depict a land with rather more woodland than we now have, fewer hedges, and large numbers of non-woodland trees.

A random selection of fifty perambulations from the *Cartularium Saxonicum* gives a total of 1,230 boundary features. Thirty-seven of these (3 per cent) were woodland, including 16 'woods', 9 'groves', and 3 spinneys or thorn groves. Fifty-three (4½ per cent) were *-lēah* names indicating sites which were, or had originally been, forest clearings. There were 6 uses (½ per cent) of 'thorn-row' or 'hedgerow' plus many instances of *haga*, which is thought to mean either a hedge or a fence. Fifty-six (4½ per cent) of the points are trees or small groups of trees (for example, 7 thorns). Nearly all of these last appear to be outside woodland; in Table 2 they are broken down by species.

The predominance of thorn as a boundary tree (sometimes with a special name like 'old thorn') contrasts with the predominance of oak in Anglo-Saxon place-names. Anglo-Saxon surveyors had an understandable predilection for rare trees. Besides lime and service, the frequent occurrence of pear is notable: many of the trees appear to have been in lonely places, and probably refer to a wild British pear now almost extinct. The regional variation is remarkable: why should so many oaks and limes be mentioned in Worcestershire, but no elders?

Evidence of place-names

Place-names are a sharp two-edged sword. Many of them date from the Anglo-Saxon or early medieval periods and can potentially provide valuable evidence about woodland and trees at a time when there is little other documentation. But despite the researches of the English Place-Name Society there are many unresolved uncertainties of date and ambiguities of meaning. The rare survival of an Anglo-Saxon charter may happen to tell us of minor place-names which we might otherwise think originated 500 years later. And does High Beech in Epping Forest, for instance, really mean High Beech or High Beach?

Place-names referring to particular kinds of tree might seem straightforward provided we avoid the pitfall of assuming that every occurrence of a tree-name implies woodland. But are places named after common trees, or after trees which were sufficiently uncommon to be notable? How many Actons (*ac* = oak) and Oakleys are so named because they contained the only oak for miles around? Is a wood called 'Birch Wood' really a hornbeam wood distinguished from other hornbeam woods by having one conspicuous birch tree at the edge?

Another ambiguity is illustrated by the *ley—wood—grove—tree* series of place-name elements. The Anglo-Saxon *lēah* appears to have had a reasonably definite meaning, a permanent glade or clearing in the Wildwood (or occasionally part of the Wildwood itself), and names, especially village names, ending in *-ley* or *-leigh* therefore imply that some of the Wildwood remained at the time they were formed. The element *grove*, Anglo-Saxon *grāf*, has almost the opposite meaning, a small, defined, and possibly managed wood, normally surrounded by non-woodland; its use therefore carries a presumption that there was not much Wildwood left when the name was formed. The implications of the word *wood* (*wudu*) are somewhere in between. *Wood* and *grove* place-names, unlike *ley* names, have of course been formed continuously from Anglo-Saxon times until now. *Tree* (*trēow*) place-names tell us next to nothing about the landscape; many areas with no woodland nevertheless have plenty of trees.

Despite these limitations, place-names if used with care can tell us a good deal about woodland and trees. Names that refer to rare trees are usually more informative than those referring to common species. Acton or Ashcroft—whatever their exact meaning—are unlikely to tell us much about oak or ash that we did not know already; but an early reference to a Chesteyns in Essex adds to our scanty medieval evidence for sweet-chestnut (page 98), while Hulver Street in Suffolk gives us a site for holly. The Domesday Book village name Linwood, Lincolnshire, reminds us of the wood of small-leaved lime which existed near by until it was tragically replanted only a few years ago.

Names referring to the destruction of woodland include Roding, Stocking, Stubbing, and sometimes Assart. *Roding*, with its variants Ridding, Redon, Reed, etc., is cognate with German *roden*, to grub out woodland, and probably with the English word *riding*, nowadays shortened to *ride*, a glade or track through a wood. *Stocking* is a place which, perhaps hundreds of years earlier, contained 'stocks', that is, tree-stumps. *Assart*, often held to have the same meaning, is really a legal term for an encroachment which, although usually at the expense of woodland, sometimes

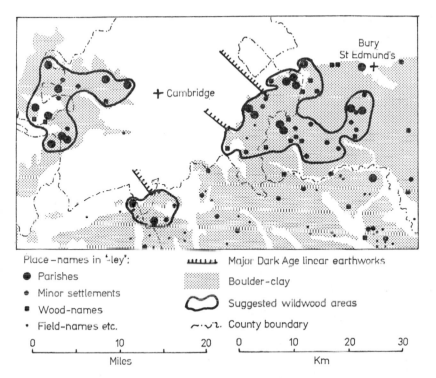

Place–names in '-ley':
● Parishes
● Minor settlements
■ Wood-names
· Field-names etc.

⊥⊥⊥⊥⊥⊥ Major Dark Age linear earthworks

░░░ Boulder-clay

⬭ Suggested wildwood areas

⌒·◡◡ County boundary

+ Cambridge

Bury
St Edmund's

0   10   20   Miles

0   10   20   30   Km

Fig. 9.   Place-names ending in the -*ley* element in Cambridgeshire and adjoining counties. Derived from English Place-name Society volumes, except for Suffolk, where they have been listed by Mrs S. Ranson.

involved heath or moorland. Brentwood, Brentgrove, and their Norse equivalent Swithenlund suggest fire in woodland, though we can no longer tell whether it refers to deliberate destruction, accidental damage, or merely charcoal-burning.

As an example of what can be done with the cautious mapping of place-names I offer the distribution of -*ley* in Cambridgeshire and adjoining counties (F g. 9). Vil age and hamlet names ending in -*ley* are strikingly concentrated on the Huntingdon-shire and Suffolk borders, suggest ng that here the early Anglo-Saxons found and colonized tracts of Wildwood that the Romans had left. In the rest of Cambridgeshire there are practical y no -*ley* names, showing that by the time the Anglo-Saxons came

57

there was no Wildwood. In much of Suffolk and Essex the -*ley*
names, although frequent, are mainly of fields and other minor
features, suggesting that the Romans left behind considerable
tracts o open land containing the villages and hamlets, with
relatively narrow belts of residual forest which were not encroached upon until late in the Anglo-Saxon period. This interpretation is supported by several other features of the settlement
pattern, and by the distribution of woods, probably fragments of
the forest, in Domesday Book and later documents. There are
also three great Dark Age dykes which cross the chalk-land, go
for about three-quarters of a mile on to the boulder-clay, and then
end abruptly as though running into forest which was thought
to require no further barrier. A similar conjunction of -*ley*
village names and intentional gaps in a Dark Age earthwork is to
be found in Herefordshire along Offa's Dyke.

Domesday Book

The several thousand references to woodland in William the
Conqueror's great survey of 1086 have been ably mapped and
analysed by H. C. Darby (1971, etc.), but their exact meaning is
difficult to discover. All official statistics relating to woodland
are bedevilled by problems of definition, and with Domesday
such uncertainties are multiplied by its remoteness in time and by
the scarcity of explanatory records for the centuries immediately
before and after. Moreover the form of the records suggests that
the commissioners were not very interested in or knowledgeable
about woods.

Domesday has six different ways of telling us about the woods
on manors. The types of record—they change abruptly at county
boundaries, showing that they are due more to the commissioners' decisions than to actual regional variations—are as
follows:

  i) Acres, typical of Lincolnshire.
 ii) Length and breadth in furlongs or 'leagues', widespread.
iii) Length only, as in part of Shropshire.
 iv) Pannage entries, 'wood for so many swine', the usual form
     in the eastern counties.

v) Swine rents, the pigs paid each year by tenants for the right to fatten pigs in woodland (*pannage*) or occasionally for the use of woodland grass (*herbage*). Entries in this form are normal in the south-east.

vi) 'Miscellaneous' entries, usually of a qualitative kind, such as 'wood for repairing houses', 'a grove for fences', etc., widely scattered but commonest in West Cambridgeshire.

Entries of the first three kinds attempt to give some idea of the size and location of woodland. Dr G. F. Peterken tells me that in Lincolnshire there is a considerable degree of correlation between the location, and even the size, of Domesday woods and the present distribution of medieval woodland or of places where medieval woods are known to have been. My own work in the Lizard Peninsula, Cornwall, shows a similar correlation.

In some areas (for example, Lincolnshire, Nottinghamshire, Huntingdonshire) a distinction is made between *silua minuta*, which almost certainly means coppice wood, and *silua pastilis*, 'pasture wood'—'wood for pannage' is a common mistranslation—which appears to have been park-like with plenty of grass. This is the first explicit record of a distinction which, as I have argued, must already have been ancient, and which was to be prominent in all later centuries.

For Lincolnshire let us make the somewhat rash attempt to reduce Domesday woodland areas to modern terms, on the basis that *a*) the woodland acre is 1.2 modern acres, as it often was in later periods; *b*) the Domesday league is 1½ miles, and the furlong ⅛ mile; *c*) on average the area of an irregular wood is 0.7 times its length times breadth. We find that out of the 1.70 million acres of the county some 58,000 were woodland. 1·3 per cent of the land area was coppice wood, 1·3 per cent was pasture wood, 0·7 per cent was 'wood pasture in places' (evidently woodland that was partly coppice type and partly pasture type), and 0·1 per cent was entered otherwise, making a total of 3·4 per cent. The 1·3 per cent cover of coppice wood seems not unreasonable for supplying what we know of the Domesday population. The pasture woods were fewer and larger; the average size of a coppice wood was 80 modern acres—somewhat above the average for later medieval woods—while pasture woods ran on average to

240 modern acres. For comparison, 2·5 per cent of the county was officially 'woodland and plantation' in 1903.

Rough and uncertain as these calculations are, they have an air of reality which we are denied in eastern England, where nearly all the entries appear as 'wood for so many swine'. There is a good deal of evidence that this relates to the practice of taking tame pigs into the woods in autumn to fatten on the acorns (or beechmast if any) before being slaughtered and salted down. Many commentators have assumed that the pig numbers are being used as a rough estimate of the size of the wood; the equation 1 pig = $1\frac{1}{2}$ acres of woodland has been suggested.

Unfortunately the matter is not so simple. Acorns and beechmast are notoriously variable crops which often fail completely. Medieval references, and a few Anglo-Saxon wills, make it clear that they were equally unreliable in past centuries. It is therefore unrealistic to expect an objective equation, however approximate, between pigs and acres. The wood-swine are notional pigs, bearing no relation to the numbers of actual animals which Domesday also gives for some counties. The assessment, however arrived at, must have depended as much on the willingness of the local pig-men to gamble on a good *pessun*, or mast year, as it did on the size of the wood.

Moreover we may question how far the practice was compatible with other uses of woodland. Pannage is appropriate to a wood-pasture situation with plenty of big oaks; but in coppice woods it may be unwanted, on the grounds that pigs damage the stools, or unprofitable, because the oak trees are too few or too young to produce enough acorns even in a good year. As the population increased and the demand for timber and underwood rose, we would expect pannage to decline in favour of other ways of fattening a pig. In 107 instances in Norfolk, Suffolk, and Essex Domesday says that the swine-assessment had decreased between 1066 and 1086. Lennard [15] pointed out that this change was not systematically accompanied by any increase in farmland and was therefore due to some alteration in the quality rather than the area of woodland. The most likely cause is an extension of coppicing; it is notable that among the places affected were Dereham, Shipdham, and Pulham in Norfolk, all of which had important woods in the thirteenth century.

Most of the swine-entries in Domesday seem to correspond to the *silua pastilis* in other counties; they refer to land used for rough grazing for cattle and sheep, with trees providing an occasional bonus of acorns for the pigs. In swine-entry counties coppice woods are recorded as such—by means of 'miscellaneous' entries—only in areas such as West Cambridgeshire where they were particularly numerous. Elsewhere they are apparently given very small swine-entries or even omitted altogether. In eastern England the big swine-entries tend to be concentrated in areas where there was not subsequently much woodland; whereas S. Norfolk, S.W. Suffolk, and S.E. Essex, with their numerous ater medieval coppice woods, have a thin scatter of swine-entries, often for only a few head or even a single pig.

The 'swine-rent' entries for the south-east are even less in touch with the real world. With the help of the Anglo-Saxon charters we know that they represent a complex branch of the Wealden economy centred around *denns*, secondary settlements often many miles from the place to which the entry applies. By Domesday many of these were long-established farming communities, whose swine-rents may well represent a 'fossilized' incident of tenure rather than an actual land use.

Despite all these uncertainties, the Domesday statistics give us some idea of the distribution of woodland in eleventh-century England (Fig. 10). In most counties there was probably much more woodland than there is now. Huntingdonshire, whose woodland adds up to about 7 per cent of the area, must have been nearer the national average than Lincolnshire with its $3\frac{1}{2}$ per cent; while Warwickshire, Worcestershire, and Staffordshire appear to have been well above the average. Nevertheless, the distribution is surprisingly familiar in many respects. Domesday records a pattern of woodland which was to endure till the twentieth century; later changes took the form of a thinning out of the pattern—more in some areas than others—more often than of a radical redistribution. Over England as a whole about six villages or parishes out of ten are recorded as having woodland, but the proportion varied widely; in Leicestershire less than one settlement in three had woodland worth recording, but in many small areas (for example, around Watford) every place had a wood. Already there were districts where a man could go many

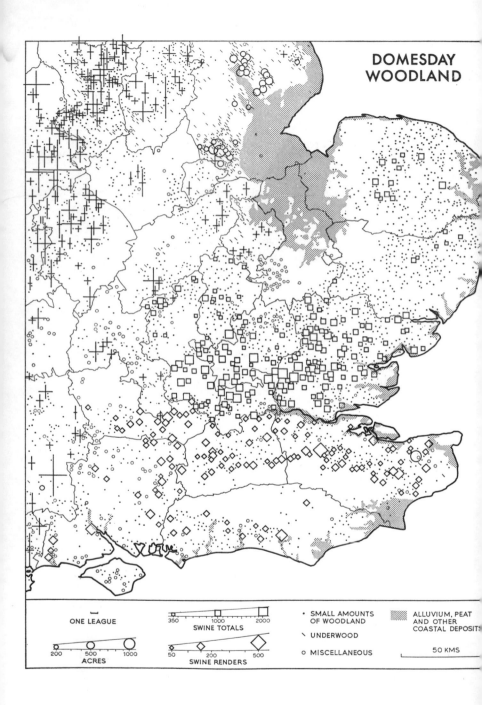

DOMESDAY
WOODLAND

ONE LEAGUE

SWINE TOTALS
350   1000   2000

ACRES
200   500   1000

SWINE RENDERS
50   200   500

• SMALL AMOUNTS
  OF WOODLAND

`\` UNDERWOOD

○ MISCELLANEOUS

ALLUVIUM, PEAT
AND OTHER
COASTAL DEPOSITS

50 KMS

miles without seeing a wood, such as the Fens, the Breckland of Suffolk and Norfolk, and the Yorkshire Wolds. Elsewhere, the landscape must have consisted predominantly of farmland with islands of wood rather than of forest with isolated clearings. Even some of the seemingly irrational local irregularities, such as the concentration of woods in three small areas of Lincolnshire, are still there today. To a large extent the distribution of English woodland in 1900, some of which still remains in 1976, was determined by forces—we can only vaguely guess at their nature —which operated before the Normans came.

In 1086 it appears that coppices, the more intensive of the two types of woodland, were widespread but still not predominant except in poorly wooded areas. The majority of woods seem to have been of the pasture type, which in the next few centuries was to decline greatly in area through conversion to farmland and coppice wood but lives on even today in the form of commons, parks, and Forests.

Contrary to popular tradition Domesday rarely names individual woods and (as far as I know) never mentions trees. To show that a wood is 'mentioned in Domesday Book' usually requires considerable historical skill, diligence, and luck. One example is Wayland Wood in S.W. Norfolk, which has a Viking wood-name (page 108). Domesday refers, not directly to the wood, but to Wayland *Hundred*, or division of the county, named after the wood, where it is probable that the hundred court was held. This was therefore a grove of assembly, perhaps even of heathen worship, long before the Conquest. This exceptionally historic and interesting wood—it is also the Babes-in-the-Wood wood, and much of its underwood consists, almost uniquely outside northern

Fig. 10. Woodland as recorded in part of England in 1086. Length-and-breadth measurements (p. 58) are represented by crosses of different sizes. Other kinds of Domesday record are represented by different symbols; the size of each symbol is proportional to the quantity recorded. The map expresses these distinctions only for the larger non-underwood woods, although the original record gives them for all woodland except 'miscellaneous' entries. The reader should not try to equate the amounts represented by different kinds of symbol. Reproduced by permission from H. C. Darby, *A new historical geography of England*, Cambridge, 1967.

England, of the bird-cherry *Prunus padus*—still happily survives intact.

Domesday occasionally gives industrial uses of woodland, such as the continuous supply of cartloads of wood to the Droitwich salt works. Disputes about woods show that they were often private property. There are rare references to secondary woodland: for nstance, the grimly evocative account of what had been eleven settlements on the Hereford-Radnor border, the scene of a frontier incident some thirty years before. 'On these waste lands woods have grown up, in which the said Osbern has the hunting and takes away what he can get. Nothing else.'

The last of the Wildwood

Domesday Book depicts a late stage in the destruction of the Wildwood. By the thirteenth century the use of the remaining fragments, either as coppice or as wood-pasture, had crystallized further, and some of the actual woods of that period still exist. A wood such as Wayland is almost certain to be primary (or conceivably post-Roman secondary); its plant and animal communities are in direct continuity with those of the prehistoric forest, without ever having had to colonize a new site. The same is likely to be true of almost any medieval wood, the great majority of which appear to be on sites that escaped forest clearance.

Ancient woods and (in different ways) wood-pastures provide our last link with the Wildwood. But they are not the same as the Wildwood, which in its natural state, experiencing no felling and relative y little grazing, must have been very different in structure and to some extent in its species. The popular myths that Wistman's Wood on Dartmoor and Staverton Park, E. Suffolk, are surviving Wildwood will not bear examination, remarkable as these places are: Staverton is a medieval deer park, and its hundreds of pollard oaks bear witness to centuries of intensive use (Peterken 1969), while Wistman's Wood has a chequered history and has much increased within living memory.[16]

The last approximation to virgin forest in England may have been in the Forest of Dean around 1150. By 1250 Dean was extensively coppiced and pastured, but this state of affairs was probably not long established (Hart 1966). On the Domesday map there is a blank, which appears to result from a real lack of human activity rather than an anomaly of recording. Between 1241 and 1265 Henry III gave 71 oaks out of Dean to make timbers for the Dominican friary at Gloucester, where they remain to this day.[17] These timbers—perhaps the last remains above ground of the English Wildwood—are very unlike those typical of later medieval buildings. They have been sawn from huge oaks, about 2 feet 3 inches in diameter at the middle and 50 feet in usable length.

Patches of virgin forest may have survived longer in Scotland and Ireland but are not adequately documented. Part of the Speyside pine woods was sufficiently remote to escape felling, and perhaps grazing, apparently until the seventeenth century (page 94).

4   Classical woodland management: the Middle Ages and after

A certain Wood called Heylewode which contains 80 acres by estimate. Of the underwood of which there can be sold every year,
without causing waste or destruction, 11 acres of underwood which
are worth 55s. at 5s. an acre. . . . A certain other Wood called
Litlelond which contains 26 acres by estimate. Whose underwood
can be sold as a whole every seventh year. And it is then worth in all
£6 10s. at 5s. an acre.

*Earliest surviving management plan of
Hayley Wood, West Cambridgeshire, dated 1356* [18]

The beginning of detailed woodland records

In the year 1251 Hugo de Northwold, Bishop of Ely, caused a
great survey to be made of the estates belonging to his bishopric.
This work, known as the *Old Coucher Book of Ely*,[19] is a minute
account of lands and tenants in dozens of parishes scattered over
eastern England. It gives the names of scores of woods with
estimates of their acreages and various particulars of their uses.
The Coucher Book begins a new era in detailed land recording. It
is immediately followed by a number of other estate surveys,
particularly on lands of the abbeys of Ramsey, Huntingdonshire,
and Bury St Edmund's; and by the Hundred Rolls of 1279, the
second, and even now the most detailed, national survey of land
tenure, though the rats have eaten most of it.

Part of the Coucher Book entry for Barking, E. Suffolk, reads:

The woods
Item, there is one small park which contains nine acres,
including a laund, measured by the aforesaid perch.* Which

* This phrase means, in this case, that the woods are measured in terms
of the modern acre (Rackham 1975).

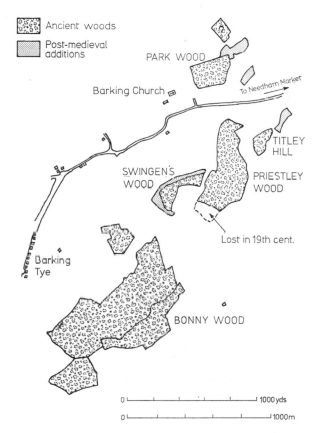

Legend:
- Ancient woods
- Post-medieval additions

PARK WOOD

Barking Church

To Needham Market

TITLEY HILL

SWINGEN'S WOOD

PRIESTLEY WOOD

Barking Tye

Lost in 19th cent.

BONNY WOOD

0 _____ 1000 yds

0 _____ 1000 m

Fig. 11. The ancient woods of Barking, Suffolk, as they are now. In the case of Bonny and Priestley Woods there exist early large-scale maps which confirm that these woods have had exactly the same boundaries for at least 350 years.

would be worth every year, including the laund, four shillings if it were not for the beasts.

Item, there is one grove which is called Tykele which contains five acres by the aforesaid perch. And a certain other grove which is called Prestele which contains thirty acres by the aforesaid perch. And a certain other grove which is called Wetheresheg which contains seven acres by the aforesaid perch. And these three groves are worth sixteen shillings every year.

Item, there is one big wood which is called Boynhey which is estimated to contain ninescore acres. It is worth £4 10s. per annum.

It is immediately obvious that this is an essentially modern countryside with islands of wood surrounded by farmland. The park and laund will be explained in Chapter 8. A glance at the map raises the suspicion that at least four of the woods are still there; for in Barking there are woods called Park Wood, Titley Hill, Priestley Wood, and Bonny Wood, which correspond roughly in acreage with those of the 1251 survey (Fig. 11). As it happens there are numerous documents from intervening centuries which confirm that this is so; indeed the missing wood, Wetheresheg, is almost certainly still in existence under another name. We see in Table 3 that the acreages agree to a surprising extent over 720 years; as is often the case,[20] the wood areas appear to have been underestimated in the thirteenth century.

Table 3. The Barking, Suffolk, woods

1251	*c. 1639*	*1974*
Parvus Parcus 9 ac.	Parke woode 14 ac.	Park Wood 14 ac.
Grava de tykele 5 ac.	Tickley woode 4 ac.	Titley Hill 5 ac.
Grava de prestele 30 ac.	Presley wood 43½ ac.	Priestley Wood 39 ac.
Grava de wetheresheg 7 ac.	Swynsey woode 13 ac.	Swingen's Wood 14½ ac.
Magnus boscus de boynhey 180 ac.	Boyney wood at least 100 ac.	Bonny Wood 130 ac.

This is by no means an isolated case. The same continuity can be shown for many other woods in the Ely Coucher Book—a well-known example is Hayley Wood, Cambridgeshire—and other thirteenth-century surveys. Roughly half the Coucher Book woods, including small ones like Titley, still existed in

1945, and so did nearly all the W. Cambridgeshire woods listed in 1279.[20]

There is no reason to suppose that the start of continuous records corresponds to any sudden change in the woods themselves. For all we know, they may have been unchanged for centuries before. We have seen some pre-Conquest examples in the last chapter, while even the tiny Knapwell Wood, W. Cambridgeshire (Fig. 19c), can be taken back almost to the Conquest (Rackham 1969).

Woodland in the medieval landscape

The closely written folios of the Ely Coucher Book describe intricate systems of multiple land use in which a number of persons had rights in different products of the same piece of land. Hardly any land was unused: the large areas of 'waste' do not, of course, mean derelict or unoccupied land, but land whose uses were communal rather than private.

By the thirteenth century the place of woodland in the English countryside was well established. Woods whose primary functions were to produce underwood and timber were differentiated, as in earlier centuries, from the various categories of wood-pasture. They were pieces of property with definite boundaries; usually they were privately owned, though some woods had common rights of various kinds. And unlike modern plantations they were permanent features of the landscape. Although woods could be converted to other land uses such as arable or wood-pasture, or vice versa, these were rare events in the life of any individual wood, and many woods (like those of Barking) were little altered by them.

The management of woods was both intensive and conservative. In the Middle Ages men expected to have to live off renewable resources, and by 1250 they managed woods on the basis that whenever a tree was felled another would grow in its place. Innumerable surveys either state a coppicing rotation for woods or give a figure for the expected annual return. Occasionally, as in the quotation at the head of this chapter, we find the self-renewal principle stated even more explicitly. Felling at short intervals of years ensured vigorous and trouble-free regrowth; woods were

69

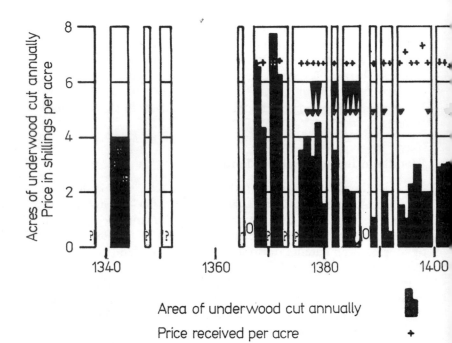

Fig. 12. Acres of underwood felled each year in Hardwick Wood, Cambridgeshire, from 1341 to 1495, together with the price per acre and the years in which timber trees (mainly oaks) are known to have been felled. O indicates an explicit statement that no wood was cut; ? indicates a year in which the manorial accounts do not mention wood, and probably also implies nil output. Gaps in the time-scale indicate missing records.

fenced to keep out cattle which might eat the young shoots. Trespasses against woodland—letting one's sheep get in, stealing acorns or underwood—were dealt with by fines similar to those imposed for other petty offences against property. A very early and somewhat graver instance of such proceedings is given on page 15.

Usually a wood boundary consisted of a bank and ditch combined with either a fence or a hedge. We hear occasionally of new

Hardwick Wood

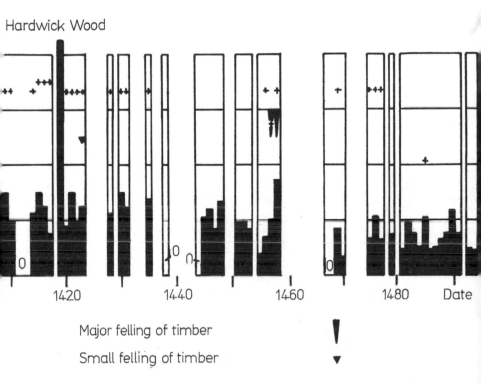

1420   1440   1460   1480   Date

Major felling of timber

Small felling of timber

earthworks being made, as for instance when a wood was sub-
divided; but there is no reason why some of them should not be
much older than 1250. For Knapwell, Cambridgeshire, the
Ramsey Cartulary refers in the early twelfth century to 'the grove
of Cnapwelle and the arable land which is inside the ditch
[*foveam*] which surrounds the grove', which suggests that even at
that early date Knapwell Wood had been reduced in size within
an earthwork that had marked its old boundary.

The records are curiously silent about woodland rides, most of
which seem to have been cut in the post-medieval period.
Previously there had probably been impermanent tracks winding
among the stools, an arrangement which survived until the
twentieth century in the large Chalkney Wood, N. Essex.

71

The management of underwood

Most medieval woods were of the type that we call coppice-with-standards. The site was shared by standard trees and underwood; the latter produced an annual return of wood, while the former yielded timber at longer and less regular intervals. More often than not, wood was the more important of the two products and the one that we hear more about.

We have seen that coppicing was well established in 1086. By 1251 it was going on in nearly all the woods covered by the Coucher Book and other surveys. Medieval woods were cut at irregular, though frequent, intervals; the average cycle was an abstract concept which surveyors did not always see fit to estimate. Felling rotations, where given, are usually short: seven years as in Hayley Wood, six years, five, or even four (as at Pulham, Norfolk). Hardwick Wood, which still exists in Cambridgeshire, was supposed in 1356 to be cut on a five-year cycle;[18] the annual statistics [21] (Fig. 12) show that while this was a good estimate of the average, the actual acreage cut fluctuated widely from year to year. In later centuries some woods, particularly those with specialized functions, were cut with strict regularity every so many years. As anyone who manages a wood will know, such an inflexible programme is not very practical. Demand for the products fluctuates, and for various reasons different parts of a wood do not always grow at the same rate, so it is often advantageous to cut more in some years than in others.

Besides written evidence about underwood, we have the stuff itself preserved in wattle-and-daub—the wooden reinforcement, embedded in hard-setting clay, used in the various wattling systems that fill the panels of the timber-framed buildings. The material consists of whole or split sallow or hazel rods or of laths cleft from oak timber, tied together with withies (one-year-old sallow shoots) or string. It is very durable and often is as good after 500 years as the day it was made. The annual rings in the rods confirm that woods were felled usually at eight years' growth or less, and show that medieval coppice grew at least as fast as it usually does now.

Medieval woodmen seem to have taken little interest in the composition of underwood, and we are not told about it systematically, although from casual references in court rolls and accounts we learn that woods were mixtures of much the same coppice species—ash, oak, hazel, maple, elm, lime, birch, crab-apple—that we find in ancient woods now.

The commonest recorded uses of wood are firewood and fencing. Firewood normally consisted of underwood or wood from other sources tied up into faggots. Fencing was an important item in an age when men seldom saw wire. One of the commonest of the many variants was a row of stakes interwoven with *ethers*—long flexible rods—either standing on its own or acting as reinforcement to a hedge. Hurdles were usually of the type that is woven from small hazel rods. There were also numerous uses in building.

This variety of uses explains why the composition of underwood did not matter much. Every kind of tree had its uses, but the more specialized underwood crafts used relatively little material, and the bulk uses of wood were for purposes such as fencing and especially fuel, for which a number of different trees could be used. Nothing of the underwood was wasted; even twigs and hedge-trimmings were faggoted up and used. On this no-waste basis, the appropriate length of a coppice rotation is determined more by taste and convenience than by considerations of biological productivity.

Fig. 12 shows how the coppice cycle in Hardwick Wood during the fifteenth century became longer (that is, fewer acres were cut each year) and more regular. This illustrates a tendency which applies also to other woods and was continued in later centuries.

Management of timber

The timbers preserved in buildings are a more valuable supplement to written records than are the underwood rods. Building was a major use of timber—written records suggest that it used over half the timber produced by woods. We must not pay undue attention to the more expensive structures such as hammer-beam roofs, which may not be representative. The cheapest buildings will seldom survive.

We live in an age which treats timber as if it were plastic. We have grown used to chain-saws, specialized vehicles, sawmills—

not to mention the machine that gobbles up standing trees and grinds them to pulp. This machinery is designed to reduce trees, regardless of their natural properties, to whatever dimensions we (I mean our timber merchants) choose. Our predecessors had to be more cunning, to select trees for size rather than cutting them to size. A building system adapted to using a certain size of tree implies a woodland system that regularly supplied it.

The following summary of practice is based on the study of a number of medieval and sixteenth-century buildings in East Anglia (Rackham 1972, 1974); the principles are not confined to that region [22], [23] but we do not at present know how widely they apply.

Oak appears everywhere to have been much the commonest *timber* tree in woods, and was used in buildings even where it must have been brought from a distance. Elm, pine, etc. occur in undoubted medieval buildings, but are uncommon before the eighteenth century.

Ordinary medieval buildings contain large numbers of small oaks felled usually at twenty-five to seventy years of age. Each timber (except of course for boards) is a whole log squared with the adze or broad-axe; sometimes, especially in the later Middle Ages, a log is sawn (rarely split) lengthwise to form two timbers. Timbers of small scantling were got by choosing and felling small trees. A high proportion of medieval timbers are impressed with the shape of the tree in which they grew. They are waney—rounded at the corners through reaching the outside of the log—or crooked; often the sapwood, and sometimes even the bark, has been left on. Carpenters were skilled in turning to good use the irregular shapes in which wild oaks naturally grow (page 128); sometimes, as in the cruck buildings of Wales and the west and north of England, naturally curved oaks were deliberately chosen for special purposes. Recent discoveries in the W. Midlands raise the interesting speculation that the cruck system is adapted to using the huge curved timbers provided by the black poplar (Fig. 6).[24]

Because of the close relation between timbers and the trees in which they grew, it is possible to decide how many trees went into a building and to a considerable extent their ages, shapes, and sizes. Grundle House, Stanton, a timber-framed farmhouse

74

typical of hundreds built in W. Suffolk around 1500, contains some 330 trees, a tenth of which are elm (Rackham, 1972). Half of these were less than 9 inches in diameter at the base; 32 trees were as small as 6 inches; while only 3 exceeded 18 inches, a usual size for a 'mature' oak nowadays. The roofs, floors, and internal walls of the mid-fourteenth-century Old Court of Corpus Christi College, Cambridge, contained about 1,400 oaks, most of them less than 9 inches in diameter. Turning to grander buildings, the fifteenth-century main roofs of Norwich Cathedral contained some 680 oaks, mostly around 15 inches in basal diameter.

The timbers of ordinary buildings are usually up to 20 feet long; those that are longer are often crooked, knotty, and tapering where they reach into the crown of a tree that was not really long enough. The high roofs of great churches are an exception in that they contain large numbers of timbers with a reasonably straight length of about 30 feet. Particularly expensive structures such as the great Perpendicular roof above the vault of King's College Chapel, Cambridge, may contain 'outsize' trees 30 inches or more in diameter. The ultimate size of post-1300 oaks is suggested by the grandest timber frame of all, the Octagon of Ely Cathedral, built 1328–42. The inner timber tower rests on 16 struts which are meant to be 40 feet long by $13\frac{1}{2}$ inches square, but with all England to draw on for the timber the carpenter evidently had to make do with trees that did not quite meet this specification. All the struts taper rapidly at the top where they reach far into the crown of the tree; in six cases the design has been altered to use trees that even so were not quite long enough. Oaks of this size are nowadays rare in woods but one does occasionally see them (Plate IV). The largest oak timbers on record appear to be 16 of no less than 50 feet long which were in stock at Westminster in 1329.[22]

This evidence from buildings agrees very well with what the records say. We are seldom given measurements of trees, but statistics of prices and of charges for felling and transport tell us something about the range of sizes. The accounts for Hardwick [21] and Gamlingay,[25] Cambridgeshire, document, year by year, the part played by timber trees in intensively managed woodland. Oak was the most valuable as well as the commonest timber tree: for instance, in 1334, the Gamlingay bailiff claimed that he had been overcharged by 2*s*. 7*d*. 'for maples which they made out as oaks in the previous account'. Oaks were very variable in size. Prices varied in the fourteenth century from 20*d*. per tree—something like £50 in the money of 1976—down to a fraction of a penny; allowing for fluctuations in the value of money the largest oaks felled from woodland must have cost about ninety times as much as the smallest.

Occasionally the need arose for oaks which were much larger than these. The post on which a windmill stood had to be *bought* at a cost of between 18*s*. and 25*s*. 1*d*., more than ten times as much as the largest oak sold from Gamlingay Wood. This post would have been about 2 feet square by at least 20 feet long (Rackham 1974); it would have weighed about 2 tons and we are not surprised to find an item for mending a cart 'which broke under the great post of the mill'.

It was the normal practice to fell a few trees each year for maintaining local buildings, machinery, bridges, and such essential items as the pound, cucking-stool, and stocks. Occasional heavy fellings took place for new buildings (Fig. 12), and in consequence the numbers of standard trees varied enormously. The 40 acres of Gamlingay Mertonage Wood supplied at least 561 trees of various sizes in 1333–7, and about 180 trees, mainly oaks, in 1358–9. Beevor (1924) gives from 5 to 40 timber trees per acre for various Norfolk woods in the fifteenth century, which provides a fair estimate of the range.

Timber was felled as occasion demanded. The carpenter would go into the wood, select and fell trees for the job in hand, and work them while still green. This practice is confirmed by occasional records of exceptions. Much of the picturesque warping and sagging of ancient buildings can be shown (on the evidence of early alterations) to have arisen soon after the frame was built, and is due to the movement of unseasoned oak as it dried.

This system was an efficient and successful means of securing a continuous yield of timber. Replacement of felled trees cannot have been a problem, else we should not find so many very small oaks used. Medieval oak timbers often have a curved butt end with a very wide first annual ring; this suggests that much use was made of regrowth from stumps, the superfluous poles from which may account for the numerous references to stakes and other very small oaks. Felling oaks young encouraged such coppice growth, gave the flexibility needed to cope with the sudden demands of building works, and avoided the heart-rots which often develop if oak stands beyond a hundred years. Complex and skilled medieval carpentry techniques exploited the natural properties of the material, and thus avoided the labour, waste, and loss of strength involved in converting crooked cylindrical logs to the precise rectangularity that modern convention demands. To use timber immediately after felling made it easier to work and reduced the problems of organization; but we may well wonder how the medieval carpenter contrived (as he undoubtedly did) to make wheels, for which precision is essential, out of green timber.

As with underwood, nothing of the felled tree was wasted. Account rolls contain entries of monies received for the bark, branches, 'loppium et chippium', twigs, and even leaves of felled trees.

Minor uses of woodland

The grasses of coppice woods, although of little agricultural value, have occasionally been exploited. *Agistment*, grazing of farm animals, was seldom permitted, except sometimes during the latter part of the coppice cycle, when little damage was likely to be done. *Herbage* seems to have been akin to the practice in Hatfield Forest, Essex, recorded in 1612, of

> reaping the Grass & carrying it away in Baggs wch would be a great hindrance to the commoners in neglect of Business of greater Weight. . . . Except it be a poor Body that hath nothing else to do . . . and he perhaps may lye in a Copice reaping grass a whole day together. . . .[26]

Pannage sometimes lingered on in woods into the Middle Ages but, like agistment, is more of a wood-pasture practice. Other woodland products included acorns and hazel-nuts (gathered by the tenants at Barking as part of their labour services), *fugerium* (apparently bracken) and bast (the inner bark of lime trees used as fibre). The bizarre German practice of burning a

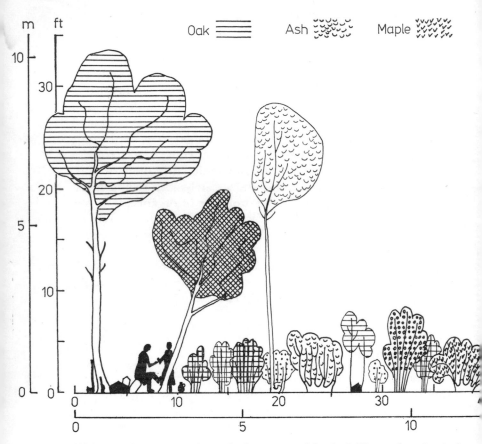

m ft   Oak ≡≡≡   Ash 〰〰   Maple ⌄⌄⌄

Fig. 13. Reconstruction of what a wood looked like under classical coppice management. Five small standard trees and a number of underwood stools (including one oak) are shown; the species are appropriate to the heavy boulder-clay soil of the East Midlands. The underwood of the left-hand half was felled last winter; that of the right-hand half has had five seasons' growth and is ready for felling again if needed.

wood after felling and growing a crop of rye among the stools (Troup 1952) seems not to be recorded in Britain.

Among sporting uses there was the curious medieval activity of cock-shooting, catching woodcock in a net strung across a re-entrant angle in a wood. A specially shaped cockshoot-wood will be seen in Fig. 15.

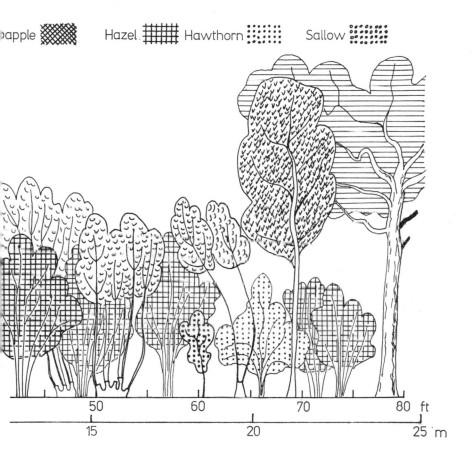

	50		60		70		80	ft

15		20		25	m

What a medieval wood looked like

A normal wood consisted of underwood of a mixture of species
cut on a short rotation. There was a variable scatter of timber
trees of a continuous range of sizes from about 18 inches basal
diameter downwards; these were mainly oak, up to 70 years old,
and chiefly of the smaller sizes. The 20-foot length which we find
in building timbers results from the growth of the underwood
suppressing the lower branches of the standard trees but allowing
them to form a crown above this height. The division between
timber trees and underwood was not sharp; the former were
often recruited from the latter, and there was probably an inter-
mediate class of large coppice poles allowed to stand for two or

79

three underwood rotations. Fig. 13 is a reconstruction of such an arrangement.

By great good fortune there still exists a working example of just such a wood. Bury St Edmunds Abbey was one of the mightiest houses of the monkish world, and until recently many of the abbey woods remained as witnesses to its pre-Reformation wealth. Felsham Hall Wood remains intact and together with the surviving part of Monks' Park (Fig. 14) forms the Bradfield Woods (Rackham 1971). Felsham Hall Wood still has its great meandering boundary bank set with pollard trees; the earthworks of Monks' Park are more complex owing to a deer park episode in its history. The underwood is still cut on an irregular and relatively short rotation, which has stood at an average of 10–11 years since the seventeenth century. Coppicing records go back to 1252. The coppice is an intimate mixture of different species: ash, maple, alder, hazel, both birches, lime, sallow, elms, etc. After cutting, the new growth sometimes reaches 10 feet high in the first year. The oaks are sparse but tend to occur in groups. Just as in the Middle Ages, they are very variable in size, age, and shape; they are quite young, and many are of stool origin. In contrast to nearly all woods nowadays, the oaks replace themselves without difficulty, and there is even a small proportion of oak coppice. There are also timber trees of other species; major

Fig. 14. Felsham Hall Wood, Bradfield St George, and Monks' Park, Bradfield St Clare, West Suffolk.

a) General topography. Felsham Hall is a typical medieval wood; Monks' Park has internal divisions which result from its history as a deer park apparently of the compartmented type (p. 147). The 'fell' names are given as in the 1850s and are now mostly different. b) Position of Felsham Hall Wood in the remotest corner of Bradfield St George parish (p. 113). Its proximity to Felsham accounts for the name (p. 108). c) The two woods as in 1700. The outline of 'Munces Park' (note the survival of the Anglo-Saxon spelling) has the characteristic 'economical' shape of the earliest deer parks (p. 144). The four internal glades, which in 1700 were meadows, almost certainly represent medieval launds (p. 146). d) Underwood in 1975. The different kinds of shading indicate the traditional patchwork of coppice 'panels' each at a different state of growth.

1 A Suffolk lime-wood, with big stools of small-leaved lime coppice of 30–40 years' growth since last felled. The smaller stools in the foreground, also of lime, were cut last season and have since made one year's growth. Groton Wood.

II Coppicing in progress in Felsham Hall Wood, Suffolk. Note the stacks of cut wood (here chiefly alder and ash) awaiting transport; the standing underwood in the background; and the thin scatter of standard trees which are mainly oaks and very variable in age, size, and branching pattern. This scene has changed very little since at least the thirteenth century.

III Underwood in Felsham Hall Wood, Suffolk, in the first autumn after felling, showing one year's regrowth of sallow and alder.

IV A big oak in South Norfolk. This tree is exceptionally large and old for an oak in a wood; it is in late biological middle age (about 260 years old) and beginning to lose branches. In the fourteenth century this would have been an outsize tree.

V Medieval (or earlier) wood-bank exposed by felling the underwood. Note the width, rounded profile, and external ditch. Felsham Hall Wood.

VI Structure of a coppice-wood after some eighty years of neglect. Beneath the standard oak-trees, the underwood has sorted itself into two distinct layers of trees: the taller, and still-leafless, 'large coppice' of ash and maple, and the 'small coppice' of hazel and hawthorn which have come into leaf.

VII A moderately large ash stool immediately after felling. It has been so treated at intervals of about ten years throughout its life. Felsham Hall Wood. *W. H. Palmer*

VIII The Felbrigg Beeches, Norfolk. Very slow-grown ancient pollards, last cut in the eighteenth century, with microscopic annual rings. This may be the northernmost native beech in Britain. The trees probably originated on common-land, but have been preserved by emparking. Similar beech pollards, on very infertile acid soils, occur in Burnham Beeches, the New Forest, Epping and (in the Middle Ages) Writtle Forest.

IX An enormous ash stool near Saffron Walden. This is all one tree, which through centuries of cutting has grown into a great ring with a hollow centre; it now bears about twenty stems around the margin.

x   Wood-pasture versus woodland; a little-used Roman road between woods in Hertfordshire. In the background is a wood, with hornbeam *stools* and oak timber. Next comes a wood-bank bearing hornbeam *stubs* remaining from a hedge. The hornbeams in the foreground, growing in the road itself, were accessible to the browsing of passing cattle and for this reason are cut as *pollards*.

xi   The grassland with trees of a deer-park. The ancient oak in the foreground is 'stag-headed' through the death of its outer branches: but it is not a dying tree, for this happened at least half a century ago, and the remaining foliage is in excellent health. Moccas Park, Herefordshire.

XII This very large pollard oak on an old boundary in Suffolk is an accidental survivor from the sixteenth-century landscape. Note that the site is turning into woodland through the invasion of elm suckers, some of which are being dug out as a conservation measure to protect this tree from being shaded.

W. H. Palmer

XIII The elms of the shrunken village of Knapwell, Cambridgeshire. The medieval village has moved away, leaving its pollard elms standing in rows along hollow-ways and in the boundaries of the former closes.

W. H. Palmer

XIV Part of the parish of Long Melford, Suffolk. Typical Ancient
Countryside with numerous large and small woods, irregular and
often small fields, and scattered farms. The area shown measures about
$1\frac{3}{4} \times 1$ mile; its historical development can be followed in the maps of
Fig. 15. Most of the features shown are of medieval origin. A map of
1613 depicts the great wood to the left and the cluster of groves in
the middle and top of the photograph almost as they are now, as well
as the majority of the hedges. The groves differ in their vegetation to a
remarkable degree, as can be seen to some extent in this picture. The
park and groves at the bottom date mainly from the late seventeenth
and early eighteenth centuries but incorporate earlier hedges and
field trees. Recent changes, though not quite as severe as in much of
Suffolk, have included the replacement of the great wood by a plantation and the destruction of some of the hedges.

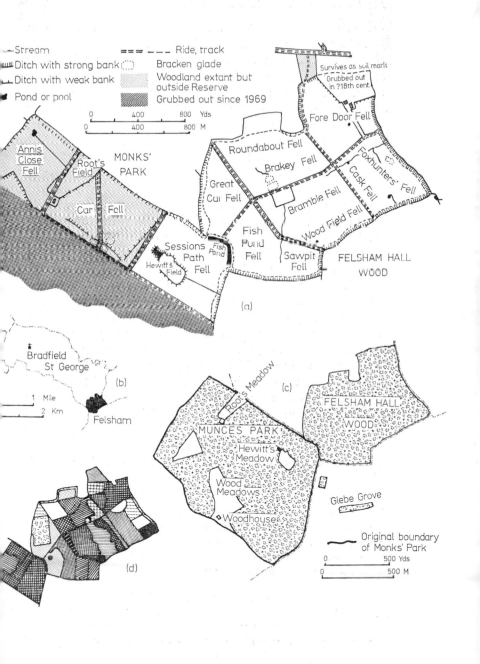

Stream
Ditch with strong bank
Ditch with weak bank
Pond or pool

Ride, track
Bracken glade
Woodland extant but outside Reserve
Grubbed out since 1969

0   400   800 Yds
0   400   800 M

Survives as soil mark
Grubbed out in ?18th cent.

Fore Door Fell

Annis Close Fell

Root's Field

MONKS' PARK

Roundabout Fell

Brakey Fell

Foxhunters' Fell

Cask Fell

Car Fell

Great Cat Fell

Bramble Fell

Wood Field Fell

Sessions Path Fell

Fish Pond

Hewitt's Field

Fish Pond Fell

Sawpit Fell

FELSHAM HALL WOOD

(a)

Bradfield St George

(b)

1 Mile
2 Km

Felsham

(c)

Roots Meadow

FELSHAM HALL WOOD

MUNCES PARK

Hewitt's Meadow

Wood Meadows

Woodhouse

Glebe Grove

Original boundary of Monks' Park

0   500 Yds
0   500 M

(d)

fellings of timber are recorded for the 1650s and 1920s. Permanent bracken glades are another medieval feature.

The Bradfield Woods are exceptionally interesting in other respects. They are among the richest of all British woods in plant life, with some 350 flowering plants recorded including 42 native trees and shrubs. This is attributable partly to their long history of continuous management, their varied structure, probable derivation from the Wildwood, and freedom from planting. Other factors are the remarkable range of soil types and the very wet site. The woods are noted also for their mammals and birds, including coppice-loving species such as the dormouse and the nightingale, their insects and fungi. Both woods survived intact into the 1960s; in 1970 the Society for the Promotion of Nature Reserves, through the energy and generosity mainly of Suffolk people, acquired most of what then remained.

How does pollen analysis, which tells us mainly about the Wildwood, link it with managed woodland? The silt of an ancient pond in Monks' Park begins to give the answer. The woods had even more plant species in recent centuries than they have now. The tree pollen is dominated by oak and hazel to a much greater extent than one would expect from the actual vegetation, but it is easy to see why these should be over-represented. Oak produces a full pollen output because it is treated as a standard tree. Hazel does so because it flowers from the second year onwards after felling. Most other underwood trees, especially lime, take several years to reach flowering size and therefore produce only a little pollen if any before they are cut again.[27]

The further value to the historian of working coppice woods is that they enable us to learn from experience about the biological, social, and economic practicalities of woodmanship. Records tell us about some aspects of the system; to learn about other aspects such as the carting of underwood one has to have worked it oneself. One cannot discover from documents the important fact that, while the trees in an underwood mixture live happily together on a short coppice cycle, once the cycle exceeds fifteen years the lower-growing species, such as hazel, tend to be over-shadowed and eliminated by their taller sisters. At Bradfield the social links still continue; the woods supply selected poles to a local factory making rakes, scythe-sticks, etc., and to other woodworking concerns, while the remaining underwood supplies the neighbourhood with stakes and firewood logs. Only the brushwood—the twigs and tops—nowadays has to be burnt for lack of buyers, although that of black birch can still be used for besoms. At all times of year the Bradfield Woods are a place of interest and delight, with the varied colours of the leaves and specially bark of the different underwood species; the strangely gnarled ancient stools; the brilliant colours of oxlip, wood-spurge, wood-anemone, and water-avens, which flourish on the different soils in the second and third springs after felling; the succession of summer flowers and butterflies; the bush-crickets chirping on hot nights; the robust ferns, stately sedges, and delicately coloured toadstools; and the aquatic vegetation of the mysterious so-called 'Fish-pond' that separates the two woods. These things remind us of the beauty and colour that went with traditional woodland management.

Although most coppice woods undoubtedly resembled Bradfield, we do occasionally hear of small groves 'of no annual value because of the abundance of big trees'.[28] These evidently consisted entirely of timber. From early times it was recognized that the more timber trees you grow in a wood the less wood you will get. In Bradfield every oak has a patch of poorly grown underwood beneath it, and it was stated in 1669 that as a result of felling 'a great part of the Timber trees' the coppice 'is become of a greater value by a third part than it was when the timber was standing'. Despite the advantages to both timber and underwood of growing them separately, the coppice-with-standards system had the advantage that it was relatively easy to maintain a continuous succession of different sizes of oaks.

Woods in society

Some of the produce of a wood was used by the lord of the manor on his own demesne farm. Some was allotted to tenants as a customary right. In Hayley Wood in 1251, for instance, each of 43 local inhabitants had the right to a specified quantity of wood each year. Such rights varied from place to place. Rights to timber or wood for specific purposes are often described as *hedgebote*, *firebote*, *housebote*, or even as *cartbote*, *gatebote*, *railbote*, *stilebote*, and 'other customary botes'. These terms sometimes define a common right to be exercised within the lord's wood; elsewhere they refer to *hedgerow* trees, which ordinarily belonged to the landlord but which a tenant might cut for certain purposes.

Not everybody, however, had rights in a wood. The ratio of wood to population varied enormously from district to district. Many parishes (especially towns) and whole districts had no woodland. And woods, however well managed, could not always be relied upon to yield the right sort of produce when it was wanted. Hence from at least the thirteenth century we find a well-established trade in timber and wood (Rackham 1975). Some was sold locally to people who had no wood rights or not enough. Some might be sent from one estate to another in the same ownership, as in 1412 when the men of Hardwick cut wood in Hayley Wood, apparently because Hardwick Wood had temporarily run out. Woodless places might get their timber from local non-woodland trees or from woods twenty miles or more away. There was also a Continental trade both in coniferous and hardwood boards. A heroic instance of the long-distance transport of outsize timbers was in 1251, when Henry III gave 30 oaks to the monks of Bury St Edmunds; they were brought from the Forest of Inglewood, Cumberland, over 250 miles away by any conceivable route.[29]

Changes in woodlands

Between 1400 and 1750 many events occurred which might be expected to have influenced woods and their management, either directly or through changes in the markets for produce. The list of pressures that come most readily to mind begins with the grubbing out of woods for expanding agriculture. There was also a rise in population, and (for some people) in standards of living; they took to living in bigger, if less solid, houses, and burnt wood in chimneys instead of on the middle of the floor. There were also 'Great Rebuildings', at various periods, of farmhouses and villages and of hundreds of timber-framed towns of which Lavenham, Weobley, and Wymondham remain as complete survivors. The rebuilding of London after the Great Fire consumed unprecedented quantities of timber and brick-making fuel.

The dissolution of the monasteries interrupted woodland organization and released second-hand timber from the demolition of monastic buildings. Capital needed to pay for monkish lands, or to meet fines incurred through religious or political misdemeanours, was most easily raised by selling timber or woodland. The close bonds between carpenter and woodman were broken as the former's skills were directed more to appearance than to structure. It became the practice in the sixteenth century to saw logs lengthwise into several timbers; this required larger, though fewer, trees, and made it more difficult to use without wastage trees that were not straight. Demands for wood as industrial fuel increased in certain areas; elsewhere the rise of hop-growing in the seventeenth century created a market for big poles.

From 1483 onwards attempts were made to control woodland management by legislation. The most important statute is that of 1543, which purported *a*) to require woods to contain a minimum of 12 standard trees per acre; *b*) to require woods to be fenced after felling to prevent them from turning into wood-pasture; *c*) to prevent woods from being grubbed out. These provisions were modelled on long-established woodland practice and were an attempt to prevent changes. Clauses *b*) and *c*) carried deterrent penalties, but the statute had so many loopholes as to be almost unenforceable; much as with modern tree preservation laws, the offender could get away with it by claiming that the trees felled had been 'seere and dead in the toppes'. This and similar Acts probably exerted their effects not through prosecutions for infringement, but by influencing the terms of leases, which they did for over 200 years.

Woods were among the most enduring and successful of all medieval institutions and proved remarkably resistant to these vicissitudes (Fig. 15). They were not in a constant state of flux. Changes took the form of modifications to the classical system rather than of radical innovations; many woods in 1900 differed only in detail from what they had been 650 years earlier.

Changes in woodland areas varied widely from county to county. At all periods some woodland was converted to farmland, especially in the sixteenth and seventeenth centuries. In Norfolk about three-quarters of the known medieval woods no longer existed by 1790. Grubbing out also occurred in the Chilterns

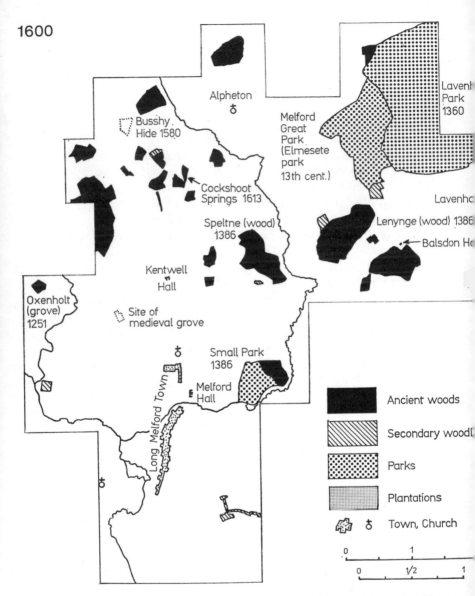

1600

Alpheton ☿

Busshy Hide 1580

Melford Great Park (Elmesete park 13th cent.)

Lavenham Park 1360

Lavenho

Cockshoot Springs 1613

Speltne (wood) 1386

Lenynge (wood) 1386

Balsdon Ho

Kentwell Hall

Oxenholt (grove) 1251

Site of medieval grove

Small Park 1386

Long Melford Town

Melford Hall

■ Ancient woods

▨ Secondary woodl

⠿ Parks

▦ Plantations

Town, Church

0   1
0   1/2   1

Fig. 15. Changes in woods and parks in and around Long Melford, Suffolk. This is an unusually well-documented area—there are, for instance, four pre-1620 maps which cover almost the whole of it—but is otherwise a typical sample of Ancient Countryside. The group of small groves towards the north-west is shown on Plate XIV.

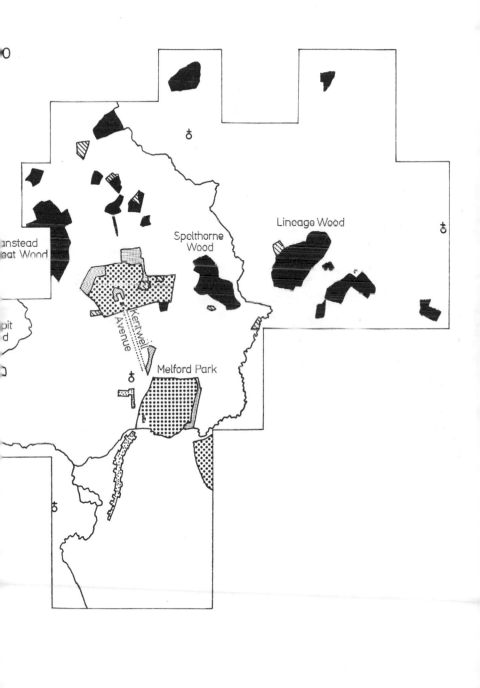

unstead
eat Wood

pit
d

Spelthorne
Wood

Lineage Wood

Melford Park

Kentwell
Avenue

1945

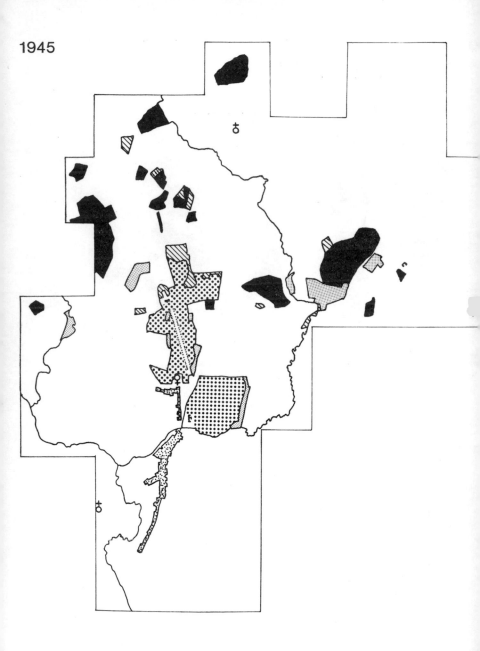

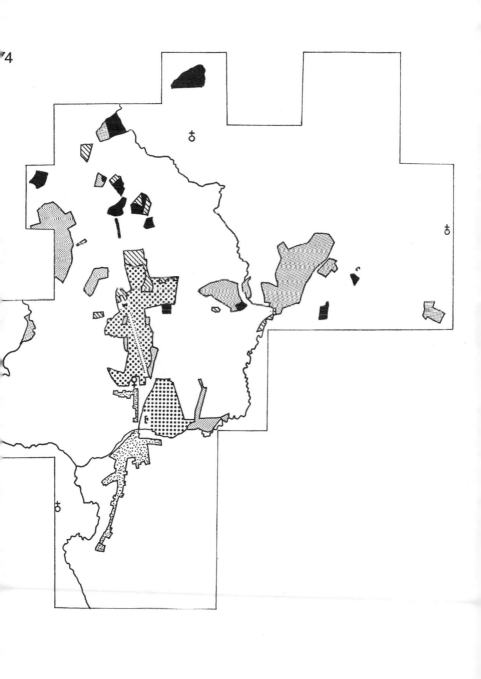

(Roden 1968) and Northamptonshire,[30] but was much less frequent in Suffolk and Essex. The process was not all one-way, for some woods increased in size, and in W. Cambridgeshire there was a gradual increase in total woodland. In the later Middle Ages, coppice woods were still being formed out of wood-pasture in the New Forest (Tubbs 1968) and the Chilterns.

In eastern England there was a strong tendency for underwood rotations to lengthen and to become more regular. The trend which we have seen for Hardwick Wood also applied to Hayley Wood, where the 7-year rotation in the fourteenth century had lengthened to 10–11 years by 1584 and to 15 years by 1765. I have evidence of over 150 coppice rotations in woods in the region; before 1400 most woods were felled at between 4 and 9 years' growth, the average being 6½ years, while after 1700 the felling interval was between 11 and 24 years, the average being 14½.

The part played by timber in woodland is difficult to summarize. In eastern England both records of woodland and building timbers show that trees on the whole were allowed to grow bigger in the seventeenth century, but there were wide variations even between neighbouring woods such as those of Barking. The continuing practice of heavy fellings at long intervals is recorded, for instance, by a survey of Little Bentley, Essex, in 1598, where the 10 woods, totalling 430 acres, mustered only 561 standard trees between them: Cowhey Wood was 59 acres (modern measure) 'wherin are but viij good tymber trees remayninge'.[31]

Eighteenth-century surveys of woods, mainly in Suffolk and Essex, show that by this time it was the practice to fell a certain proportion of the timber trees at every fall of the underwood, according to a predetermined plan, rather than irregularly as need arose. On big estates with many woods the coppice rotation was often arranged for the estate as a whole, rather than for each wood separately as had usually been done earlier. In consequence a quite large wood might be felled all at once, as was Dodnash Wood, Bentley, E. Suffolk, in 1663, 1740–1, and 1761.[32]

The history of woodland economics has seldom been adequately studied. It is useless to compare figures taken haphazardly from different parts of the country; owing to the cost of labour and transport, which could easily amount to more than the value of the standing tree, it is unlikely that prices in, say, Bedfordshire ever affected woods in Essex. Even where we have a series of figures for a single wood, it is difficult to tell whether small changes in the annual return are due to changes in the market or to changes in production occasioned by such factors as an increase in the number of timber trees at the expense of underwood.

In W. Cambridgeshire—a compact and poorly wooded district —the annual return from *underwood* on a 100-acre wood rose from about £3 in 1290 to about £110 in 1815, but most of this was of course due to inflation (Rackham 1975). The real return, measured against the Brown-Hopkins cost-of-living index,[33] rose about 2½-fold in 500 years. There was apparently a slight fall in the fifteenth century; most of the rise occurred between 1550 and 1650. In Cambridgeshire, the cost of a cubic foot of oak *timber* (including a transport element) averaged 1·5d. in 1338,[22] 1·6d. in 1500 1530, 5d. in 1560–1580, 7d. in 1590–1600, and 11d. around 1690.[34] In relation to the cost-of-living index the most important rise was one of 30 per cent between 1540 and 1553, for which there is no obvious explanation.

In Cambridgeshire, therefore, the value of woodland products tended on the whole slowly to rise, and the ratio between timber and wood tended to shift slightly in favour of wood. It is not surprising that the area of woodland slowly increased but that woodland management altered very little.

The influence of London as a wood market is perhaps shown by surveys of Crown woods between 1604 and 1612. The annual return from *wood* on 100 acres of woodland was between £7 5s. and £12 5s. in most counties, but in Essex and Hertfordshire it was £20–£23.[35]

Woods and heavy industry

The influence of industry on woods deserves to be considered further because of the almost universal belief among historians that felling for fuel has been a chief cause of destruction of British woodland. Examples of one kind and another are quoted from Roman times until World War II. The proposition is nearly always stated as a vague generality, unsupported by estimates of the acreage involved or by evidence of what exactly happened to specific woods. It is inherently implausible, for trees grow again, and a wood need no more be destroyed by felling than a meadow is destroyed by cutting a crop of hay.

The most important industry in this context is the charcoal iron trade, which had been established in many areas in the Middle Ages and had already occasionally been blamed for destroying trees. The industry reached a peak in the seventeenth century and thereafter declined, overlapping in the mid eighteenth century with the rise of the coke iron industry. This decline is popularly attributed to the exhaustion of the fuel supply. Having consumed the southern woods the ironmasters turned farther afield, and finally—it is alleged—committed economic suicide in the flames of the remaining woods of Scotland, Ireland, and the Lake District.

Little is known of how individual works organized their fuel supplies, but the national situation has been ably analysed by Flinn[36] and Hammersley.[37] Ironworks burnt charcoal, which was made mainly from underwood, although timber could be used at the extra expense of chopping it up, and had to be got locally because it was too fragile to transport far. A blast furnace working on the basis of non-renewable fuel would have taken only a few years to devour the woods within reach and would then have gone out of business. The records of furnaces, though scanty, suffice to show that they were not such fly-by-night enterprises. Half the known sites remained active for at least fifty years and a third for more than a century, which they could have done only if their fuel had been renewed in that period. Ironworks were often set up by woodland owners to run on a continuous basis in conjunction with particular coppices, as in 1541 at Pickering, N.E. Yorkshire.[38] Hammersley shows that the decline of the industry was not due to economic suicide—there is no evidence that the price of standing wood was ever more than a small part of the total costs—but to competition from Sweden with its better ores and cheaper labour.

There is little evidence that the ironmasters did reduce the area of English woods. Brandon, for instance, shows that the fragmentation of the Sussex woodlands was due to medieval agriculture long before the heyday of the iron industry.[39] Why, then, were they persistently accused of doing so by politicians and the public at the time? The answer lies partly in the over-reaction of a public which (then as now) thought all trees were irreplaceable. But there were also genuine conflicts of interest when industrialists took over woods that were already being used for other purposes. Ironmasters would not have been popular if they bought up wood supplies at prices which the local inhabitants were unused to paying, or discouraged the growth of timber trees which took up space that might have been growing wood. Matters would have been made worse by the infrequent but conspicuous practice of getting wood from commons where it would not easily regenerate.

We should mention the opposite thesis, that iron and other industries preserved and even created woodland. The polemical writer Yarranton says in 1677 that landowners around the Forest of Wyre were in the habit of planting new woods, 'knowing by experience that the Copice Woods are ready money with the Iron Masters at all times'.[40] Whether or not this claim can be substantiated from other sources, industrialists had the strongest possible interests in encouraging woodland. Most well-wooded parts of England and Wales have an industrial history. The woods did not disappear from the industrial Weald or Furness, or the Forests of Dean or Wyre, but they did vanish from agricultural Norfolk. As Hammersley puts it:

> Ironmasters ... did not plough up woodlands or uproot them, neither did they nibble the young shoots; most of them wanted to protect their investment and maintain their profits, and that needed fuel for the future as well as the present.

Scotland and Ireland

The history of woodmanship is very largely confined to the Lowland Zone. In Wales and northern England, and especially in Scotland and Ireland, stone and peat have done much of the traditional work of timber and wood, and records of managed woodland are sparse and late. Such Wildwood as remained in the Middle Ages rapidly decayed via wood-pasture; by tradition, to which the pollen record lends some colour, this process was assisted by the rise of the Cistercian sheep ranches in the twelfth century.

As regards Scotland, Anderson (1967) gives many scattered references to woodland and trees in the Middle Ages. There are a few allusions to regular woodcutting and to industrial woods, but it is clear that woodland management did not then exist on anything like the English scale. Coppicing eventually became widespread in Scotland in the eighteenth century. Tittensor (1970) describes the earliest known large-scale instance, in the Loch Lomond woods. Coppicing appears to have been established there by the iron industry in the seventeenth century; the remains of bloomeries are still to be found in the woods. The woods outlived the closure of the ironworks and were then used for various other purposes. They had been derived partly from Wildwood and partly from former farmland. As with other highland woods, both timber trees and underwood were predominantly oak, tan-bark being a major product. Attempts, not very successful, were made to remove underwood of unwanted species and to thin the oak poles. The woods were felled on a strict cycle of 24 or 21 years. There was a good deal of planting of oaks of English origin.

The Scottish pine woods are a special case. Nothing is known of their extent before the seventeenth century, when according to Steven and Carlisle (1959) they were scattered over the Highlands much as they are now. Probably they had been little used before that period. A pollen diagram by Dr Hilary Birks from Abernethy, Inverness-shire,[41] shows that that pine wood has had a continuous and remarkably unchanging history of pine dominance ever since the early post-glacial. The woods were officially 'discovered' around 1600 and heavily exploited until well into the nineteenth century. In most cases the trees felled replaced themselves from seed, and while there is some evidence of reductions in area most of the seventeenth-century woods still exist. Sir T. D. Lauder in about 1830 found in Glenmore, Inverness-shire, giant decayed trees that had escaped felling, probably the very last time that this characteristic Wildwood feature was seen in these islands.

As regards Ireland, Dr Eileen McCracken (1971) estimates, from rather vague descriptions, that an eighth of the country was 'forested' in 1600. Most of the native woodland had disappeared by 1800, although important, and relatively little known, woods such as those of Killarney remain to this day. McCracken documents the large number of trees cut down by the Irish and especially by the exploiting English, but hardly establishes that these fellings were excessive, nor does she quote sufficient local studies to explain why the trees failed to grow again. In the seventeenth century Ireland was an exporter of timber, but the quantities—5,000 tons a year at most—fall far short of unreasonable exploitation.

McCracken makes only two direct references to coppicing. Either the practice was never widespread in Ireland or there is a lack of written evidence. The latter possibility is suggested by references to 'underwood' in the Civil Survey of 1654–6 which, unfortunately, are not separated statistically from wood-pasture and scrub. The English ironworks expanded into Ireland in the seventeenth century; 13 out of 130 works are known to have operated, at least intermittently, for over a century, which must mean that they renewed their fuel supplies. McCracken's claim to the contrary is based on contemporary complaints which, perhaps, are no more to be taken at face value than are the parallel complaints in England. According to Edlin[42] oak coppices still exist in Wicklow.

5 The woods in decline: post-medieval changes

The high Price of Coal ... undoubtedly tends to increase the Consumption of Wood for Fuel ... for though it is not large Timber which is consumed in that way, but Underwood and the Branches of Trees, yet the additional Demand for Underwood renders it more valuable, and the Growth of great Trees, by which it is injured, is the more discouraged. The Inducement to the wasteful Practice of lopping Trees is, by the same means, increased. ... In Consequence of the Improvement of Roads, and Increase of Inland Navigation, the Use of Coal has, of late, become more general than it formerly was.

House of Commons Journal, 1792, p. 281

The rise of modern forestry

Although orchards and free-standing trees have been planted in Britain from Anglo-Saxon times, *forestry* plantations appear to be a post-medieval introduction. Until recently most of the theory and much of the practice originated in Germany; the earliest conifer plantations are recorded at Nuremberg in 1368.[43] Scotland, with its lack of local woodmanship, probably took up plantations on a very small scale around 1500 (Anderson 1967). In England there are a few pre-1600 instances, the earliest known being the oak plantation, attributed to Lord Burghley in 1580, which still stands in Windsor Great Park. In 1611 Arthur Standish published the first English forestry pamphlet, *The Commons Complaint*, followed by two others in 1613 and 1615. Being mainly exhortatory they are of little value as evidence; but some of the practical details, such as propagation and pruning, seem to be derived from actual experience. John Evelyn, the most eminent of Standish's successors, combined a lifelong enthusiasm for trees with considerable practical experience and a mastery of English

96

prose. His *Sylva* (1664) was a best-seller, a standard work for 150 years, and the subject of endless plagiarism; although it deals with wider aspects of trees it is in the matter of plantations that it was most influential.

In the seventeenth century plantations were mainly a gentleman's hobby rather than a serious business. Most seem to have been small compared with medieval woods; among the few known to survive are parts of Felbrigg Great Wood, Norfolk, established by the Windhams.[44] There appears to have been a steady expansion until after 1850. In Scotland, and probably in Ireland (where planting was enjoined by statute), the area of plantations overtook that of native woods at some time in the eighteenth century, a state of affairs not reached in England until much later.

Many early plantations were coppices, made in imitation of existing woods by sowing or planting a mixture of trees such as 'mast of oke, beech and the chats of ashe, bruised crabbes'. But there was an increasing tendency towards planting for timber only and towards using just one or two species, often conifers or other foreign trees. Plantations and woods therefore diverged into two different land uses, each going its own way and often appearing separately in the records.

The planting of coppices went on, at least in a small way, well into the eighteenth century and even beyond. It has often been alleged that the woods of almost pure hazel, which are widespread in southern England, are all of planted origin. Only locally has this view been supported by any convincing archaeological evidence. Against it there is a map dated 1618 showing Cranborne Chase—that stronghold of hazel woods—having almost all the woods that it now has, plus others that have disappeared, already organized as a system of coppices.[45] The planting hypothesis is not altogether implausible, although one may well ask why anyone planting underwood should limit himself to hazel rather than other species with a wider range of uses.

The first two centuries of modern forestry had little effect on existing woods. The eighteenth century was an age of much tree destruction, but mainly, as we shall see, on wood-pasture and non-woodland sites. Woods continued to be grubbed out for farmland, though not to any great extent for new plantations;

and a considerable but unmeasured acreage of secondary wood-land was formed both by intention and default, especially in and around parks (Fig. 15). Most ancient woods, however, went on performing their medieval functions of supplying local needs of timber and wood, largely unremarked by writers on the new forestry but amply recorded in the humbler pages of surveys and wood-sale accounts. Scores of Cambridgeshire and Essex vil-lagers each year bought logs and poles from their local wood.

Elms and sweet-chestnut

Ancient woods, if unchanged in area, sometimes changed in composition. Elms and sweet-chestnut tended to increase.

The increase of woodland elm, mainly by natural or at least unintentional processes, appears to have been chiefly in eastern England. Medieval documents infrequently refer to elm as a woodland tree; but from 1650 onwards new elm woods have become established by suckering from adjoining hedges, and exist-ing woods have been invaded by elm suckers (page 132). While this by no means accounts for all woodland elm it is part of a general rise of elm in the countryside throughout at least the last ten centuries. Elm invasion still goes on; Dutch Elm Disease has so far made little difference.

Sweet-chestnut is said to have been introduced by the Romans, a view supported by pollen evidence and by finds of charcoal. Even a cursory survey of medieval records shows that it occurred before 1500 in several areas where it is now abundant (Fig. 16). In the Forest of Dean it was valued in the twelfth century for its nuts and possibly its timber; its excellence as underwood seems not then to have been appreciated (Hart 1966). The famous Tortworth Chestnut in Gloucestershire is an enormous stool probably of medieval origin; other such stools occur in Hol-brook Park, E. Suffolk (page 29). Chestnut grows readily from seed (contrary to some popular opinion) and is capable certainly of surviving and probably of invasion. Although it was a favourite with writers such as Evelyn and has undoubtedly been much planted in the last 300 years, when it occurs in a medieval coppice such as Chalkney or Norsey Woods in Essex, it deserves to be considered as a possible Roman survival.

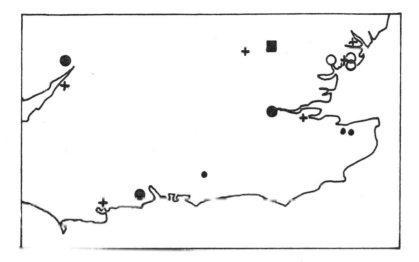

Fig. 16. Sweet-chestnut before 1500. Big dots: explicit medieval records. Small dots: sixteenth-century records which imply long establishment. Open circles: medieval *chesteine* place-names. Crosses: ancient trees (some recorded as such in the eighteenth century). Black square: charcoal found in excavation in medieval context.

The shipbuilding period

The British believe that the history of woodlands has been dominated by the influence of the sea. A nation with a proud seafaring history naturally supposes that the supply of ship-building timber has been the reason either for the sacrifice of its ancient forests or for the maintenance of its ancient woods. Although R. G. Albion collected much useful information on the subject into *Forests and Sea Power* (1926), it has hitherto been difficult to decide from published sources how much truth there is in this tradition.

The idea that shipbuilding was a steady influence down the centuries, touching nearly every wood in the country, is based on a stream of forebodings or complaints of shortage of naval timber extending from the mid sixteenth to the mid nineteenth century. But is is hard to reconcile with more specific evidence. As a major consumer of timber the shipbuilding industry was

99

short-lived. There was not much technological advan betceween the fifteenth century and the decline of timber shipping in the 1860s, but the total tonnage increased enormously at the end of this period (Fig. 17). Merchant shipping expanded with the development of intercontinental trade in the eighteenth century, while at each successive war there was an arms race which permanently increased the size of the Royal Navy, culminating in the final escalation of the Napoleonic Wars. Despite minor uncertainties about what exactly a ton of shipping meant, how much timber it took to build, and how long a vessel lasted, the conclusion seems inescapable that roughly half of all the timber shipping ever built in Britain was launched between 1800 and 1860.

Except for masts, ships were built almost entirely of British timber, most of it oak. Foreign oak was not extensively used until about 1803 and the Navy continued to rely on British oak until 1860. Some ships were captured from the enemy, and some timber was re-used from older ships; 47 these factors will be offset by the practice of adding new timbers to an old ship to supplement rotten ones. (The popular myth that ship's timbers were re-used in buildings—even far from the sea—has hardly ever been authenticated by proven examples.) The size of the fleet therefore gives a rough notion of the relative rate at which shipbuilding consumed British oak. The industry tended to use large trees (especially for warships) and had particular requirements for natural bends for making curved timbers; for this reason oak from parks, hedges, etc. was preferred to that from woods.

Early complaints about shortage must reflect poor organization or transport, or low prices offered, rather than actual lack of trees. Had there been the slightest physical difficulty in finding timber for the tiny fleet that defeated the Armada, it would have been utterly impossible to build the sixty-fold larger fleet that defeated Napoleon. Even such obvious sources as the New Forest and Dean appear not to have been touched by the Navy until well into the seventeenth century (Tubbs 1968, Hart 1966). In the eighteenth century, despite many forebodings of crisis, the reports of parliamentary commissions do not portray an industry that was being driven to substitution, economy, or even the avoidance of waste. No war was lost for want of shipping; the Navy continued to increase even after it had gained total supremacy at Trafalgar.

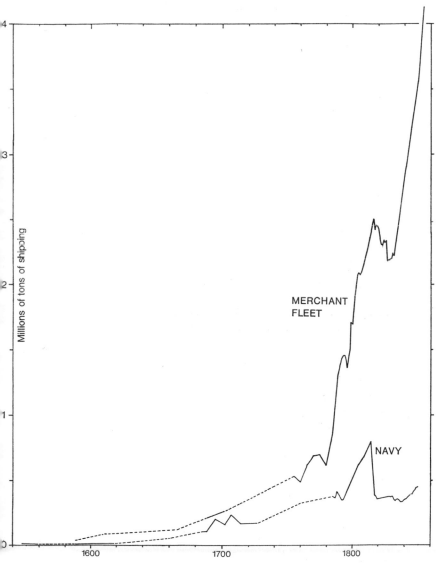

Fig. 17. Growth of the British timber-built navy and merchant marine.[46] Broken lines indicate periods during which figures are available at intervals of more than ten years.

Naval timber was cheap; the contract price remained unchanged from 1752 to 1795, although the value of money fell, and subsequent price rises merely kept up with inflation. In 1808 it was proposed, not unreasonably, to maintain even the then inflated Navy comfortably and indefinitely from 100,000 acres of plantations, less than a tenth of the woodland area at that time, to be established for the purpose. Only in 1809 did substitution begin in earnest with a large purchase of Albanian oak from Ali Pasha, despot of Yannina; and only after 1815 did the price of naval oak increase in real terms.

What permanent effects has the shipbuilding era left? The tradition that it destroyed woods is implausible (only very rarely did a wood consist wholly or largely of suitable trees) and there is no evidence that this ever happened. The economic influence of the dockyards was not universal. In Suffolk and Essex, the ratio between the prices of underwood (which had no shipbuilding use) and of oak remained remarkably steady from 1730 to 1830; and even in 1810 local users of oak could easily outbid the Navy.[32] However, the industry did provide a use—or the hope of a use—for oak between 1780 and 1860, when imported softwoods were replacing it for building purposes. This may well have saved woods which would otherwise have been grubbed; but by encouraging landowners to grow oak it hastened the decline of the ancient co-existence between different uses of treeland, the official contempt for which is illustrated by the passage at the head of the chapter. This change is best documented for wood-pasture in the Forests (page 156); but in some coppice woods also we find a change from the traditional scatter of oaks to a close-set stand beneath which a remnant of the underwood makes shift to survive.

The decline of woodmanship

Documentation generally becomes poor in the latter nineteenth century, but is supplemented by the evidence of existing trees. Coppicing fell into decline: many woods ceased to be felled from 1870 onwards, although the majority were still managed until after 1900.

The reasons for the decline of woodmanship have not been

critically studied. In the Chilterns, as early as the eighteenth century,[48] the coppices were replaced almost entirely by the practice of growing timber beeches on the selection system widely practised in semi-natural forests on the Continent (Roden 1968). Elsewhere it has not been general for coppicing to be supplanted directly by a rival management practice. The Victorian forester often planted trees in existing woodland but seldom deliberately destroyed the underwood. Woods in which coppicing ceased fell into silvicultural neglect.

The decline of coppicing is connected with the loss of its ancient markets. The firewood trade was severely undercut by the coming of the railways, chiefly from 1840 to 1870, which introduced cheap coal to the countryside. Wood industries, although badly organized and having no spokesmen in high places, showed remarkable vitality as late as 1900. Successive editions of *Kelly's Directory* show that in East Anglia the number of specialists in rakes, hoops, and hurdles actually increased until 1908; they must have competed successfully with metal substitutes. Had there been a National Woodlands Board able to command capital, mechanization, subsidies, and research, there is little doubt that some modification of woodmanship would still flourish. Unfortunately it was universally misunderstood either as being a primitive form of forestry, or as depending on specialized and supposedly obsolete crafts. All available funds and development skills were poured into plantations instead.

The first nation-wide survey distinguishing coppice woods was made by the Board of Agriculture in 1905, and shows them as covering 1·65 per cent of England (about a third of the total area of woods plus plantations), 0·33 per cent of Wales, and 0·12 per cent of Scotland. Coarse as these figures are—who can tell when an abandoned wood ceases to be a coppice?—they are worth mapping (Fig. 18), for no better record survives since Domesday, and in all subsequent surveys the ancient woods have been split up among different categories and cannot be disentangled. Already we see the tendency of coppicing to retreat from the north, which has continued ever since.

A Scottish survey of 1845 separates 'natural woods' from 'plantations'. The former, although incompletely recorded, can be estimated as 0·91 per cent of Scotland.

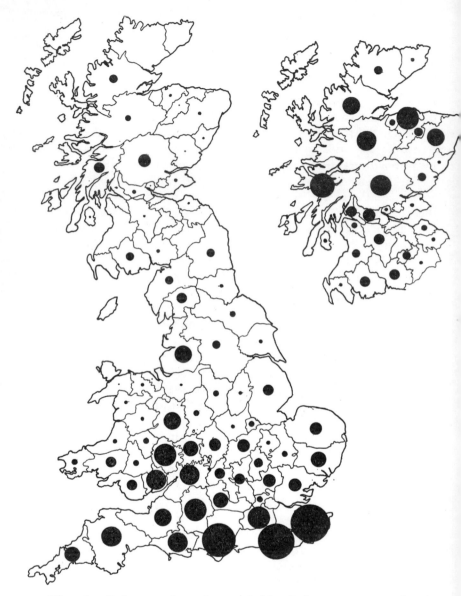

Fig. 18. Left, area of woods regarded by their owners as coppices in 1905. From Board of Agriculture returns. Each black circle is ten times the area which the woodland for the county would occupy at the scale of the map. Right, area of 'natural woods' in Scotland in 1845 shown on the same basis. Computed from information in Anderson (1967).

The first half of the twentieth century

This period saw a further decline in what was left of the traditions of woodland conservation. In the nineteenth century the nation had got into the habit of obtaining its cellulose by plundering other countries' Wildwood. When this activity was unexpectedly interrupted by German submarines the Government's reaction was to encourage the growing of conifers at home, a policy put into effect by the Forestry Commission founded in 1919. Most of the new planting was on moorland or heath, and the policy might have had little effect on ancient woods had it not been decided that they, too, were appropriate places for growing conifers. The decision to treat existing woods as if they were moorland, and the failure of academic foresters to recognize them as a distinct land use, were to discourage any attempt to revive woodmanship and ultimately were to destroy many woods.

A great deal of timber was felled to meet the sudden needs of two world wars. Probably even more was felled in the social upheavals between the wars, when a quarter of England changed hands in four years and landowners often found themselves in sudden need of capital. There is little evidence for the common belief that these fellings led to much diminution of woodland. Many plantations turned into low-grade secondary woodland after felling. Ancient woods rarely disappeared from the map, and often—as in Hayley Wood, Cambridgeshire (Rackham 1975)—the felling restored a balance between timber and underwood that had been upset by nineteenth-century encouragement of oak. Even woods 'devastated' by clear-felling, such as Monks' Wood, Huntingdonshire (Steele and Welch 1973), have grown again from the stools and have suffered little permanent harm. These fellings were not a total departure from normal woodmanship; often they were the last occasion when it was exercised. Of course a large minority of woods escaped such fellings altogether.

A number of natural and semi-natural events have left their mark on surviving woods. In 1908 there was the first report of oak mildew, a supposedly introduced disease,[49] which perhaps goes some way towards elucidating the much debated problem of why oak does not now grow readily from seed in woods: oak may be less tolerant of shade if it has mildew to contend with as well. A more certain catastrophe was the unprecedented plague of caterpillars which struck oaks throughout Europe from 1916 onwards; in Hayley Wood at least a quarter of the oaks died and are still lying about. The Dutch Elm Disease outbreak of the 1930s had some effect on woods, but owing to the great capacity of elms for repairing damage traces of this are now hard to find except in the annual rings.

In the last seventy years birch, which had been present in the lowlands throughout historical times, has become much more prominent. It has invaded woods after felling and has formed secondary woodland on derelict fenland, felled plantations, and abandoned wood-pasture. The parallel expansions of sycamore, chiefly into highland woods, and of *Rhododendron ponticum* in the south and west, go back into the nineteenth century. Among animals, fallow deer now roam the country as they have never done before, and can be a serious hazard to coppicing. The rabbit, which had escaped from semi-domestication in a similar way in the eighteenth century, was locally destructive of underwood, but the chief consequence of its sudden decline through myxomatosis in the 1950s has been a rapid increase in scrub, invading many types of old grassland to form the secondary woodland of the future. Grey squirrels, however disastrous to hardwood *plantations*, are less of a nuisance in woodland, especially as their habit of stripping the bark from sycamore prevents the latter from getting out of hand.

Unprecedented as these vicissitudes were, they did not apply equally to all woods. In 1945 there were undoubtedly thousands of woods which still retained a substantial degree of continuity with their medieval vegetation; some hundreds, mainly south of the Thames and in East Anglia, were still within a coppice rotation. Loss of woodland, by physical destruction of the stools, is mainly a phenomenon of the third quarter of the twentieth century.

6 Woods as we now see them: a guide to field-work

Ancient banks will be rounded, and consolidated by centuries of drumming rain, and of baking sun.
They may be worn down, but they will not be crumbled by modern traffic, either two-wheeled or four-footed.

*   *   *

Where such banks are continuous, they will be slightly rambling in alignment, and their corners and turns will be gradual and rounded.
Ancient banks will be broad, as a general rule.

Heywood Sumner, *The ancient earthworks*
of the New Forest (1917)

Principles of the archaeology of woods

The methods of woodland archaeology are closely akin to those used in the study of churches and other standing buildings. Woods, like buildings, may have been in constant use for many centuries, and have accumulated natural changes and deliberate alterations down the years.

With woods, as with buildings, only a small part of the evidence is simple and direct. Detailed maps and the absolute dates provided by counting the annual rings of living trees go back (for woods) some 400 years. Most other evidence involves a geater or lesser amount of circumstantial interpretation of a kind widely employed by archaeologists in other fields. The objective is to investigate in what respects features such as earthworks and vegetation patterns are historically determined, and where possible to construct chronologies for them. This may be based on written evidence, as for instance when one compares woods with a continuous documented history since the Middle Ages with others known to have originated in the eighteenth century.

Or it may depend on internal evidence, particularly that provided by alterations, as when a wood contains earthworks of two types which intersect in such a way as to prove that one earthwork is the more recent. A combination of written and internal evidence may be called for in the case of a wood which, though known to be medieval, partly overlies the ridge-and-furrow earthworks produced by ancient ploughing. Once a provisional chronology has been established from woods which have a good historical record or contain clear evidence of alteration, it can be applied to the interpretation of other sites which are not so favoured.

The woodland archaeologist is advised to make simultaneous use of as many lines of inquiry as possible. An argument involving vegetation and earthworks is generally more convincing than one based on vegetation alone. Written evidence should be used wherever possible because the dates which it provides afford a means of escaping the Charybdis of circular argument which awaits the investigator who confines himself to field evidence.

The names of woods

It is not uncommon for woods in England to have their own proper names that are almost as old as those of the surrounding villages and hamlets. A few wood-names are recorded in the Anglo-Saxon charters and Domesday Book, though men seldom had occasion to set them down in writing until the thirteenth century. The forms of these early names often have the same characteristics of Anglo-Saxon and Norse vocabulary and grammar that we find in the names of settlements, and show that the woods themselves were already separated and named in that distant period when such forms were in common use. Wayland Wood, Norfolk, anciently *Wanelund*, is an example of the Old Norse wood-names based on *lúndr*, a grove or sacred grove (Smith 1956). An Anglo-Saxon parallel is *fyrth*, a wood, which has given rise to many Frith or Frithy Woods. Anglo-Saxon case-endings, dating from the time when English was an inflected language like Latin, are preserved in the old spelling of Felsham Hall Wood (Fig. 14). *Ffelshamhalle* is, as its name implies, the wood 'at the Felsham corner' (*hale*, dative of *halh*, a corner)—the corner nearest Felsham of Bradfield St George parish.

The Norman-French language is represented among wood-names by *coppice* and *copse*, usually synonymous, which of course imply a particular form of management. The English equivalent is *spring*, which often appears as the name of a small wood with coppice management. *Hurst* can mean any isolated grove, especially one on a hill, but is often applied to series of defined coppice woods attached to parks or common land, like the 'hursts' in Sutton Coldfield Park, Warwickshire. A wood that was itself common land gives rise to the name Manwood or Mangrove.

Apart from *Spinney* (a wood of thorns) and *Carr* (a wood of alders) early wood-names seldom tell us much about the composition of woods. A wood consisting of a particular kind of tree is implied by the Anglo-Saxon ending *-ett*; but names like *Birchet* and *Oket* are much less common than their French equivalents *Biolet* and *Chesnaye* or the German *Birchat* and *Fúchat*. In Lineage Wood in Long Melford (Fig. 15) we are tempted to suspect a rare survival of a pre-Anglo-Saxon wood-name. The medieval spelling *Lenyng* suggests a derivation from Celtic *lem*, elm; and (until recently coniferized) this was one of the largest elm woods in England, dominated by a non-suckering elm that on biological grounds is unlikely to be a recent invader.

Many woods are named after the village, hamlet, or farm to which they belong. *Hayley* Wood in Cambridgeshire perpetuates the name of a deserted settlement near by, and the name of Man Hall, a manor in Little Chesterford, Essex, has been transmuted into *Emanuel* Wood which overlies its remains. Some woods, now called after parishes, had names of their own in the Middle Ages: Hinderclay Wood and Pakenham Wood, W. Suffolk, used to be called Stanberowe and Leinthenhale. In areas where woods are numerous they tend to be named after their owners or tenants, but such names are seldom kept up to date; Peverel's Wood near Saffron Walden, Essex, is still called after a family not heard of in the parish since Domesday Book.

Maps and surveys

Accurate large-scale maps begin, although infrequently, around 1580 and from then on provide a continuous stream of evidence.

They usually depict parishes or parts of parishes—occasionally single woods—at scales of 1:10,000 or larger (frontispiece). Large-scale cartography appears suddenly as a fully developed art. Maps of all periods vary from the diagrammatic to the highly accurate; late ones show no appreciable improvement on good early ones. The accuracy of any particular map can be checked by using features that survive in modern maps and aerial photographs. A high proportion of seventeenth- and even sixteenth-century maps are almost equal, both in quality of surveying and

Fig. 19. Medieval woods and later alterations. The original boundary of each wood, if extant or (as in e) and h)) surviving as a field boundary, is shown by a thick line; a thick broken line shows an original boundary that has disappeared altogether. No account has been taken of recent coniferization in a), d), and g).

a) Chalkney Wood in Earl's Colne, Essex. Sinuous outline unaltered, save in one small detail, since map of 1598 [51] (frontispiece). b) Kingston Wood, Cambridgeshire. Complex zigzag outline, largely unaltered since map of 1721,[52] with moated manor-house (probably on the site of an independent Anglo-Saxon settlement) in the middle. c) Knapwell Wood, Cambridgeshire, first recorded *c.* 1130; d) Lumpit Wood in Glemsford, W. Suffolk (first recorded 1251). Very small but complete medieval woods with boundary-banks and boundary pollards. e) Woods at Hintlesham, E. Suffolk. A trio of woods with complex sinuous and zigzag outlines, shown on a map of 1595 [53] and since altered both by addition and subtraction. The strip of secondary woodland across Hintlesham Wood is on the site of a 'prospect avenue' cut through it during the landscape-gardening period. f) Middle Wood in Offton, E. Suffolk. Although there is no early map the earthworks strongly suggest two additions to the original very sinuous outline. It was called 'le medilwode' in 1481 but seems even then to have been the only wood left in the parish. g) Gamlingay Wood, Cambridgeshire. Unaltered since map of 1601.[54] From at least the thirteenth century it was divided into two parts belonging to different manors: the dividing earthwork still exists but has had no function since the manors were amalgamated in 1599. h) Hinderclay Wood, W. Suffolk. A medieval wood reduced to a rectilinear shape by encroachments; the original boundary is reconstructed from eighteenth- and nineteenth-century maps. i) Bourn and Longstowe Woods, Cambridgeshire. j) London Jock in Widdington, Essex. Almost unaltered since map of 1635.[55] Avoids streams on two sides.

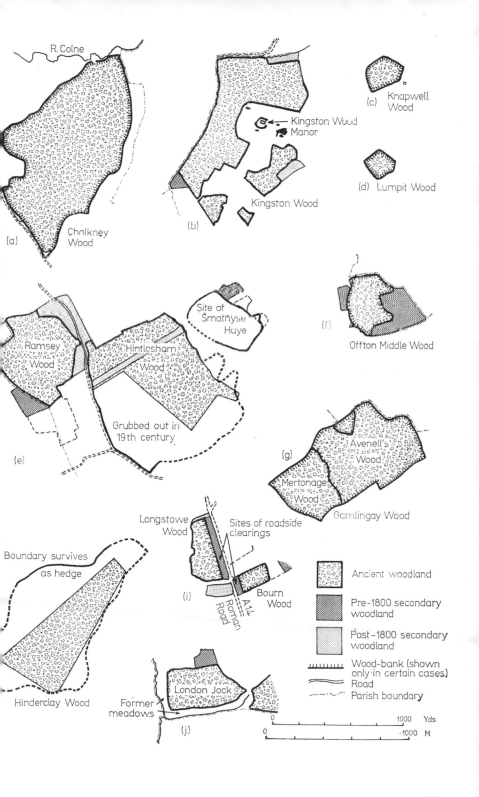

R. Colne

(a) Chalkney Wood

(b) Kingston Wood

Kingston Wood Manor

(c) Knapwell Wood

(d) Lumpit Wood

(e) Ramsey Wood   Hintlesham Wood

Site of Smathyse Haye

Grubbed out in 19th century

(f) Offton Middle Wood

(g) Avenell's Wood   Mertonage Wood   Gamlingay Wood

Longstowe Wood   Sites of roadside clearings

(i) Bourn Wood   A14   Roman Road

Boundary survives as hedge

Hinderclay Wood   Former meadows

(j) London Jock

Ancient woodland

Pre-1800 secondary woodland

Post-1800 secondary woodland

Wood-bank (shown only in certain cases)

Road

Parish boundary

0   1000 Yds
0   ·1000 M

in detail shown, to the 25-inch Ordnance Survey of the 1880s which represents the zenith of large-scale map-making.

The frontispiece shows part of a huge map of the parish of Earl's Colne, Essex, made at a scale of 1:4750 by Israel Amey in 1598. The wealth of detail is typical of some of the earliest reasonably accurate maps. The outline of Chalkney Wood should be compared with Fig. 19a.

The art of making small-scale maps, at 1 inch to the mile or smaller, developed much more slowly. Few county maps earlier than 1750 are of any use to the woodland historian. The large county maps, such as Chapman and André's Essex, of the period 1750–1820, often leave out known woods (especially those away from roads), and their wood outlines, when checked against contemporary large-scale maps, prove to be wildly inaccurate. Successive maps of this type often copy one another. In all these respects the early Ordnance Survey now in the British Museum is little better, whether in its published version or in the surveyors' drafts, often embellished with fictitious field boundaries. After 1820 the Ordnance Survey shows a rapid improvement, but it is not until the mid nineteenth century that small-scale maps attain the same degree of reliability as large-scale ones.

Verbal surveys, which go back well into the Middle Ages, often provide evidence of the exact location as well as the names and sizes of woods. The perambulation of Hatfield Forest, Essex, in 1298, for instance, mentions only one wood, Rowewode, and there is still a Row Wood at precisely that point on the boundary.[50]

The sites of medieval woods

Ancient woods tend to occur in particular places in relation to the local topography. In East Anglia and Essex the great majority are on high ground, usually on hilltops or broad ridges. The next commonest location is on slopes greater than about 1 in 10, especially if they contain springs. The large areas without ancient woods include the Fens, the Breckland, and the flood-plains and gravel terraces along big rivers. Woods tend to have been formed, and to have survived, not so much on sites that are good for growing trees as on sites that are bad for anything else.

No ancient woods are to be found on river terraces, fens, or riverside meadowland, all of which were valuable for other purposes. Woods survive on flat clay hilltops which were difficult to drain, and on slopes too steep or too wet to cultivate. *Large* tracts of poor land tended to become moors or heaths, with or without trees.

Ancient woods tend also, though with many exceptions, to be in remote places, on parish boundaries and often in the farthest corners of parishes. Although they usually occur away from villages, they often have single houses attached to them. These may be mere woodwards' cottages, but often a substantial moat indicates a house of some importance (Fig. 19b).

Medieval woods in the lowlands seldom abut directly on rivers or large streams, or on main roads. The avoidance of streams (Fig. 19j) is presumably because in those days well-watered land was so valuable that even the narrowest strip of it was worth making into meadow. Exceptions are in places where the stream valley is steep-sided. Main roads are avoided because, in an age of rural crime, local authorities encouraged landowners to remove objects from alongside roads which might afford cover to gangsters intending to attack passers-by. In 1284 a statute laid down that underwood and wood-banks should be removed for a distance of 200 feet from main roads. A number of thirteenth-century roadside clearings still survive, as along the A1 in Huntingdonshire. In other cases—like Bourn and Longstowe Woods, Cambridgeshire, where a murder was committed on Ermine Street (now the A14) in *c.* 1280 and clearings were made in the hope of preventing a repetition[56]—the wood has encroached on the road again but the old wood-banks survive (Fig. 19i). Such clearings, dating mostly from the thirteenth century, provide strong evidence that a wood then existed, but the converse does not necessarily hold; Dunmow High Wood, Essex, is a well-documented medieval coppice, but comes right up to a main Roman road with no trace of a clearing.

The shapes of woods

The earliest large-scale maps show beyond doubt that many wood outlines were exactly the same (to within a few feet) 400 years ago as they are now. Changes, if any, have involved the addition or subtraction of definite areas. Almost every wood shown on such maps, if it survives at all, has retained at least part of its ancient boundary; and more than half the *smaller* surviving woods are still exactly the same shape as they were in the sixteenth century. The maps of the Long Melford, Suffolk, area (Fig. 15) provide many examples. Where a wood has increased in size, the old boundary nearly always survives as an internal earthwork. Where part of the wood has been grubbed out, the old boundary often remains as a hedge or a soil mark running through the fields (Figs 14, 19).

Ancient wood boundaries—those shown on the earliest maps, or specified in medieval documents—have characteristically irregular outlines. Two types can be recognized: *sinuous* shapes, in which the boundary straggles across country in a series of curves with changes of direction every few yards, and *zigzag* shapes with abrupt changes of direction at rather longer intervals (Fig. 19). Sinuous outlines are commoner and, with practice, can be used to pick out possible medieval woods on the 2½-inch map.

These outlines are responsible for much of the beauty of woodland in the landscape, but are emphatically not the result of the aesthetic movement. Many of them are in places where they cannot readily be seen. Although landscape designers sometimes imitated such shapes when setting out groves in parks, eighteenth- and nineteenth-century wood boundaries run characteristically in straight lines, or less often in regular curves such as circles and ovals.

Early wood-margins tend to avoid streams and other natural features and seldom pay any regard to drainage considerations. They date from a period when the landscape was laid out on the ground rather than in the draughtsman's office, and when the countryman saw no purpose in straight lines. In Planned Countryside the outlines of medieval woods sit awkwardly among the rectilinear fields that the enclosure commissioners had to fit in round them. In Ancient Countryside, although the whole field pattern is less regular, many wood outlines are more erratic even than the field boundaries that abut on them. Some of them probably date from the forest clearance period. We may conjecture that sinuous

114

outlines were determined by the need to go round individual large trees, for instance if a tract of Wildwood was being demarcated into a wood-pasture and a coppice wood portion. Zigzag outlines may result from successive small intakes of farmland from the forest. A re-entrant angle may represent the point at which some Anglo-Saxon peasant laid down his twybill after a season's assarting, never to return because of pestilence or the Danes.

A perfectly straight edge usually indicates a wood boundary later than 1700. There are a few exceptions: in Dodnash Wood, E. Suffolk, the straight edges appear on a map of 1634[57] and have earthworks of medieval type.

Boundary earthworks

In lowland areas, apart from stone-wall country, nearly all woods more than 100 years old have some kind of earthwork round the edge. Typically this consists of a bank and ditch, the bank being on the *wood* side. As we have seen, boundary earthworks have been a normal feature of coppice woods since the Middle Ages. They exist in several types; their interrelations can be established from wood boundaries known from written evidence to be of different dates, from boundaries left behind by the enlargement of a wood, and from places where banks of different date intersect.

Medieval wood boundaries normally have relatively massive banks and ditches partaking of the characteristics of ancient earthworks quoted at the head of the chapter. In one exceptional case, Norsey Wood, Billericay, S. Essex, the unusually substantial boundary earthwork even has a name—The Deerbank. Profiles vary considerably (Fig. 20); the normal shape is rounded, but there is a broad flat type which seems to be associated with woods connected with early deer parks. These early earthworks are usually at least 30 feet in total width. Very rarely one meets a known early wood margin that has no bank or a 'reversed' bank (on the outside of the wood). In some parts of England reversed banks are particularly characteristic of *park* boundaries (Crawford 1954). Wood-banks follow all the irregularities of both the sinuous and the zigzag types of boundary; this is why even complex outlines are so stable, for any straightening out

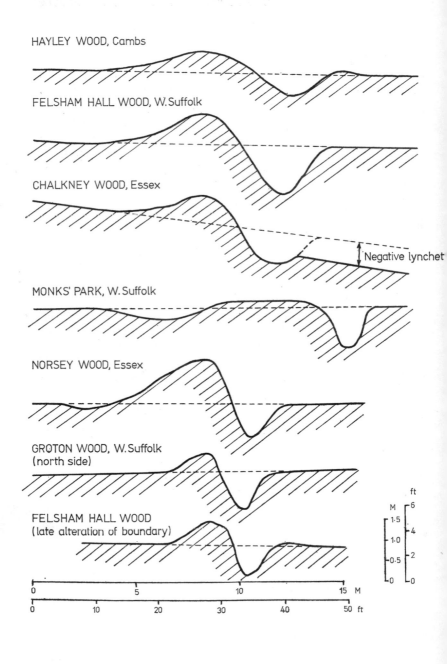

HAYLEY WOOD, Cambs

FELSHAM HALL WOOD, W. Suffolk

CHALKNEY WOOD, Essex

Negative lynchet

MONKS' PARK, W. Suffolk

NORSEY WOOD, Essex

GROTON WOOD, W. Suffolk
(north side)

FELSHAM HALL WOOD
(late alteration of boundary)

M	ft
	6
1·5	
	4
1·0	
	2
0·5	
0	0

| 0 | 5 | 10 | 15 M |

| 0 | 10 | 20 | 30 | 40 | 50 ft |

involves a lot of earth-moving to efface the bank. Where a massive bank turns a sharp corner there is a corner mound formed by the earth cast up from both sides of the ditch.

Wood-banks formed in later periods are progressively less massive and more acute in profile. They continued to be formed into the nineteenth century, by which time the typical wood-margin, like the field hedges of that period, is perfectly straight, with a small ditch and bank of triangular profile bearing a single row of hawthorns.

Outlines and earthworks can be used to reconstruct the history of alterations to a wood for which precise documentary evidence does not survive. Fig. 19t shows an embanked wood of very irregular shape inside later additions; a document of 1628 suggests that the large eastern addition to the wood had already taken place. Multiple banks and ditches around a wood may tell of successive encroachments of the wood on adjoining land, particularly on roads. Road-narrowing, politely called 'purpresture on the highway', is a time-honoured, and still by no means obsolete, method of winning an extra strip of land. In one Suffolk wood I have counted five successively diminishing parallel banks between the wood and what is left of the lane alongside!

Where a wood abuts on arable land we often find a change of ground level. Some readers will call this a type of *lynchet* because it is caused by ploughing, accompanied perhaps by soil erosion, moving earth towards, or away from, the boundary. It is most often seen on sloping ground on light soil and is, naturally, more pronounced the older the wood boundary. Usually we have a 'negative lynchet' (Fig. 20) where soil has been moved away from the wood; where a field lies up-slope from a wood we may get a 'positive lynchet' of soil accumulated against the wood edge.

Fig. 20. Measured profiles of wood-banks. Hayley and Felsham Hall: medieval boundaries on level ground. Chalkney: medieval boundary on a slope. Monks' Park: one type of deer-park boundary, with faint internal ditch. Norsey: probably derived from a deer-park boundary. Groton and Felsham Hall: boundaries created by seventeenth- or eighteenth-century encroachment on medieval woods. The wood side of each boundary is shown on the left. The vertical scale is exaggerated twofold.

Other surface features in woods

We do not plough our woods and seldom dig in them. They tend to preserve all the earthworks and other surface features that there have been on the site since it became a wood, subject to minor disturbance by felling and tree-roots. Faint earthworks are best looked for in late February, when the ground vegetation has died down, and the worms have eaten the more palatable of the fallen leaves.

Apart from boundary banks, the commonest earthworks specific to woodland are drainage grips. True drains—many ditches in woods originally had some other function—either take a straight course along rides or meander among the trees. Often there is a branching system of very small channels without banks laid out with much skill in following the lie of the land, incorporating natural streams and earlier earthworks, and using pre-existing ponds as sumps. Most grip systems are in level woods with little natural drainage, but their occurrence is haphazard, as one would expect of a practice that depended entirely on the whims of individual owners. They appear to be mainly post-1750 and later than the woods in which they occur.

Saw-pits and charcoal-pits were usually temporary and filled in immediately after use. Few examples survive in this country; they should be looked for in places where they could be dug without filling with water. Saw-pits should be regular rectangles; charcoal (more often made above ground in a stack or kiln) requires an accurately circular pit.

Earthworks resulting from non-woodland activities can include practically anything: hill-forts (numerous along the Welsh Border), linear defensive ditches, barrows, trackways and Roman roads, castles, deserted settlements, moats, and hedge-banks. In some cases the connection is incidental; but often the earthwork is the reason for the existence of the wood because it provided a bit of uncultivable land on which woodland developed. Many small groves in arable country, which the passer-by dismisses as nineteenth-century pheasant coverts, turn out to contain barrows or moats; in the case of moats, as we shall see, it is possible that the trees are an integral part of the history of the site.

Some of these features are compatible with pre-existing wood-

land. The ancient mine-workings of the Forests of Dean and
Wyre and the medieval and later industrial reservoirs made by
damming valleys in the Weald and the Black Country may often
have been formed inside existing woods. But many types of 'non-
woodland' earthwork can only have arisen on open land. When
they occur in a wood they prove that the site is secondary woodland and set a limit to its possible age. A useful feature of this
type is *ridge-and-furrow*, the round-topped parallel undulations
which result from long-continued ploughing. Classical ridge-and-
furrow results from the ploughing of strips in medieval open
fields;[58] it consists of ridges between 5 and 12 yards wide, 140 to
260 yards long, typically about a foot high, and gently curving
(often with a 'reversed-S' double curve). Ridge-and-furrow was
also formed in enclosed fields, sometimes as late as the nineteenth
century: late examples are straight, narrower and sometimes
longer than the medieval kind. Ridge-and-furrow is widespread
in former open-field districts, but is not universal. It was also
produced by the *run-rig* type of open field practised in some Celtic
areas. If correctly identified, it always indicates secondary woodland, but its absence does not prove that a wood is primary.

The countryside contains innumerable pits, ponds, and depressions. We know something of the uses to which these have been
put, but little systematic study has been made of their origin
(which may be unrelated).[59] Certain well-defined categories of
artificial pit—for example, gravel-pits, brick-pits, and marl-pits—
sometimes occur in what is now woodland. Ancient woods are
often full of mysterious depressions for which it is difficult to
invent such an origin; for instance Wolve's Wood, near Ipswich,
in 90 acres contains at least 26 deep pits and ponds plus count-
less shallow hollows. Such features are irregular and apparently
random in shape and nearly always negative (pits, not mounds).
Particularly in boulder-clay, they may well originate from such
natural processes as the melting of masses of ice in glacial times.
A concentration of natural hollows may be one of the obstacles
to cultivation that have caused particular sites to be set aside as
woodland. Hollows are less noticeable outside woods: the
shallower ones have been ploughed out and the deeper ones are
indistinguishable from other kinds of field pond.

A potentially useful historical record is provided by soil

structure. A heathland episode, for instance, may generate an iron pan in the soil which persists even if the site later becomes woodland. Such evidence has sometimes been applied [60] to arguments about continuity of 'tree cover' (for example, at Staverton Park, Suffolk, Peterken 1969). But there is plenty of room for disagreement among experts about how soils can be expected to develop under particular combinations of geology, climate, and vegetation.

Plants and animals as part of the history of a wood

Every wood is a highly complex series of communities of plants and animals. Such communities are constituted, for instance, by the trees and shrubs; the flowering-plants and ferns growing on the ground; the birds and other larger animals; the mosses and lichens growing on trees; and the armies of fungi and creeping things which live off various kinds of rotting plant remains. These interdependent plants and animals reflect the history of the site to varying degrees. This historical link may result from *continuity*. A newly established wood, for instance, does not suddenly acquire all the characteristic woodland organisms; some get there within the first few years, while others, incapable of travelling long distances, may still be missing centuries later. Conversely, heathland converted to woodland does not suddenly lose all the characteristic heathland species. A second historical link depends on *management*, for instance on the effects of coppicing, pollarding, or grazing. Historical links may also be provided by *development of the habitat*, such as accumulation of leaf-mould and changes in the soil profile.

Not all organisms are useful as historical indicators. We shall deal chiefly with flowering-plants, including trees, which have been quite well studied and will mean something to the general reader. Similar relations have been found in other groups of animals and plants, which unfortunately will be familiar only to specialists. Many insects, and several slugs and snails, are regarded as 'old-woodland species', and some spiders and mosses may behave similarly.[61] Lichens present a particularly interesting case, contrasting in many respects with flowering-plants, which will be discussed under parks. Mobile creatures, such as most mammals and birds, should be able to settle down wherever a suitable habitat presents itself; their historical significance, if any, can only be indirect.

Woodland structure and related matters

Woodland structure is the most useful single source of information about what has gone on in a wood during the lifetime of the existing trees. It can easily be appreciated by the amateur, who can recognize coppiced or planted trees without much botanical book learning, although to understand the finer points is an art in which one's experience grows over the years.

The shape of a tree that has been coppiced—a stool base with two or more main trunks—is normally unmistakable in all trees that are capable of coppicing, except for hazel, woodland haw-thorn, and sallow, which grow naturally into such a shape. Coppice structure is still perfectly plain in many woods that have not been cut for a century or more, and can still be recognized in a wood that has been converted to 'false high forest' by cutting out all the poles but one on each stool. The coppice structure is not equally strong in all ancient woods; the stools can be destroyed, wholly or partly, by grazing, replanting, or elm invasion. Occasionally one can confuse sparse coppice stools with casual regrowth from the stumps of timber trees, or with the oaks and beeches that sometimes branch near ground level in woods that have arisen spontaneously on heath or downland.

Pollards and stubs in a wood generally stand on boundaries, often, but not always, in conjunction with boundary banks. Sometimes they mark obsolete divisions that have had no meaning for at least 200 years. Pollards which make no sense as boundary markers usually indicate an episode of wood-pasture (for example, common or parkland) in the wood's history, as in The Mens, Sussex.

One of the ways in which we can decide whether a wood has been planted is to look for trees in rows, but these are not as easy to identify unambiguously as one might suppose. A single tree-row may be due to chance alignment or to natural establish-ment along the line of a ditch or ride-edge, while occasionally a regular pattern may be imposed on the vegetation by soil features such as ridge-and-furrow. Aerial photographs are useful but should not be trusted without confirmation; under certain conditions they may fail to show up real tree-rows or may give the illusion of rows that are not really there. Of course, the absence of rows does not indicate that there has been no planting. Nor does the presence of rows prove that the wood is merely a plantation; it may contain trees that survive from before the planting or that have arisen since.

A minimum limit to the age of a wood is normally given by the age of the oldest trees in it. Annual rings can sometimes be counted in dead trees or in the stumps or abandoned branches of trees felled half a century ago. Occasionally we find trees that are obviously older than the wood in which they grow, as with the giant slow-grown park- and common-land oaks—much older than the ruined Georgian mansion—among the recent birches of Thorndon Park, S. Essex.

In many woods the oldest trees are the coppice stools. The age of the poles tells us when the wood was last coppiced; sometimes we can find the half-rotten stumps of the previous crop of poles which tell us how long the last rotation was. The age of the stools themselves (page 29) is a guide to the minimum age of the wood. As usual, hazel is less informative than other underwood species. Giant stools, of course, indicate ancient woodland, but in some ancient woods, particularly on acid soils or in the Highland Zone, they are few or absent. The commonest cause of death of stools appears to be overshadowing by timber trees. Woods such as Felsham Hall, W. Suffolk, in which underwood has always been more important than timber, may have large numbers of big stools; while in other woods nineteenth-century planting of large numbers of oak or ash for timber has all but eliminated the giant stools.

Stumps and dead trees may tell us much about the last two centuries. The poorly preserved coppice structure of a known ancient wood, for instance, may be accounted for by the stumps of an unusual number of standard trees which shaded the underwood in Victorian times but have since been felled. Dead trees, or trees showing recovery from damage, may record past catastrophe by lightning, caterpillars, or disease. Or they may result from natural competition, as when oak is overtopped and gradually killed by beech or elm (page 33).

Variation in tree communities

Many native woods are not uniform in their tree communities. The underwood, for instance, may vary from an ash-hazel mixture in one part of a wood to a maple-hazel mixture in another part and to pure hornbeam in a third (even though the timber trees will usually be the inevitable oak throughout).

Wholly artificial variation, due to the planting of blocks of different trees, is easily recognized because of the abrupt and usually straight boundaries which often coincide with rides, fences, etc. At the other extreme, much variation—more often in underwood than in timber trees—appears to be almost wholly natural, due to the intrinsic properties of the trees and to their reactions (present or past) to soils and other aspects of the environment. Natural variation is often gradual and subtle, as with the complex underwood changes in the Bradfield Woods. Often the trees and the herbaceous plants vary together, and sometimes the cause can be diagnosed. In Hayley Wood aspen tends to go with abundant oxlips; both are favoured by spring flooding (though it has taken considerable research to show this), but for quite different reasons, and hence the correlation is not perfect. Sudden changes in woodland can arise from natural features such as spring-lines; and there are naturally gregarious trees, for example, hornbeam and small-leaved lime, that tend to occur in patches with abrupt edges. Natural transitions, whether sharp or gradual, are irregular, eschew straight lines, and disregard management boundaries.

There are also historical variations which are partly natural and partly artificial. There may be differences of structure and composition between an ancient coppice and a recently wooded area alongside; between a coppice and a former wood-pasture; or between a wood invaded by elm and an area which the elms have not yet reached.

The floras of ancient and recent woodland

It is observed that woods with a long history, and especially ancient coppice woods, generally have a richer flora than recently established woodland, and contain certain characteristic plants which the latter lacks. Continuity, management, and development all contribute to this difference. The ancient wood, if primary, will have inherited species from the original Wildwood; if secondary, it will have had sufficient time to acquire all but the least mobile plants. The recent wood will have acquired only those plants which readily colonize new sites or which survive from the previous land use. Moreover the plant communities of the ancient wood will have had perhaps a thousand years in which to come to terms with management, often with the mixed-coppice system which provides a series of habitats favouring a rich and complex flora. The continual cycle of felling and regrowth provides a home for plants with varying requirements for shade, while the mixture of tree species ensures that some areas, for instance under ash trees, will always be suitable for plants that cannot stand heavy shade. Recent woodland, whether natural or planted, is usually more uniform in structure, all parts being equally and often densely shaded.

I shall resist the temptation to draw up a rule of thumb for woods like the well-known 'one shrub species per century' for hedges. A wood acquires plants faster and less evenly than a hedge. On average one might guess that a wood of between 10 and 200 acres having 20 native trees and shrubs and a total of 150 flowering-plant species is likely to be at least 400 years old. But such an average is not very useful. The number of plants one finds in a wood is liable to be disturbed by many factors, for example, soil composition and variety, neglect or maintenance of coppicing, broad rides on which grassland can persist, and not least by how long one spends looking for them. Poolthorn Covert in N. Lincolnshire, dating from 1797, owing to a favourable combination of such circumstances has a richer flora[62]—though not in plants specific to woodland—than the hursts of Sutton Coldfield Park, Warwickshire.

Species lists are thus a poor archaeological guide. It is more useful to look for individual species that characterize woods with a particular type of history. To illustrate the method, let us look at a well-known example, the Oxlip, *Primula elatior* (not to be confused with the 'false' oxlip, a hybrid between primrose and cowslip). This plant is confined in Britain to a well-defined area in Cambridgeshire, Suffolk, and Essex. Within this area it occurs in practically every wood known on documentary or topographical grounds to be ancient. It often grows in great abundance but is hardly ever found outside such woods. In several cases this plant has spread into secondary woodland adjoining a primary wood; observations at Hayley Wood suggest that it does so at the rate of some 4 feet a year. But in only 4–5 out of over 100 sites is it known to have jumped across a few hundred yards of open country to colonize an *isolated* secondary wood. There are numerous secondary woods, some of them more than 350 years old, that fail to contain it. Significantly, the oxlip is extremely rare in hedges; in Hayley Wood there used to be 4 million oxlip plants, yet not one grows in the ancient hedges that abut on the wood.

The oxlip is not a unique instance. Other plants behaving similarly in East Anglia include the Woodland Hawthorn, Wild Service, and Herb Paris (*Paris quadrifolia*). From a careful study of the Lincolnshire flora G. F. Peterken (1974b) has identified 50 plants more or less confined to primary woodland, including such a common species as Wood Anemone. Such plants nowadays find difficulty in colonizing new sites, although they can survive indefinitely in existing sites. Among possible reasons for this difference may be mentioned climatic changes which may prevent them from setting good seed; changes in woodland structure; and the extinction of animals which may once have served to disperse the seed. But above all, for a thousand years our woods have been discontinuous. Plants can no longer move in short stages through continuous forest; to reach a new site involves a jump across farmland.

An interesting case is the small-leaved lime, which we know from the pollen record to be a living link with Mesolithic times. Nowadays it has difficulty in growing from seed—probably the modern climate is against it—and, as befits a relict from the Wildwood, is strongly associated with ancient woodland and seldom grows in hedges. (Of six hedgerow occurrences in Suffolk, three are in hedges which once were wood boundaries.)

We must use this method with caution. In this, as in other respects, plants vary in their behaviour from one part of the country to another, and although some species, such as small-leaved lime and woodland hawthorn (*Crataegus laevigata*), are associated with ancient woodland widely in Britain, this is not always so. Bluebells, for instance, in Suffolk usually go with ancient woods on acid soil. In Cambridgeshire they occur on alkaline soils as well and get into the older secondary woods. Near the west coast they are not confined to woodland at all. Moreover even the more exacting woodland plants occasionally survive in habitats that are not woodland. A railway cut off a corner of Hayley Wood in 1863 and made it into grassland; oxlips, bluebells, and anemones all survived out in the open and are still there 114 years later. This perhaps explains the occasional records of oxlips in wet meadows. The oxlip in Britain is on the edge of its geographical range. Although it has little power to colonize new sites, it survives with tenacity where it already grows provided it is protected from grazing, ploughing, and the competition of ranker herbs. It grows in woods because it needs protection, not shade; and occasionally, as in meadows and along railways, it lives under the protection of the scythe rather than the axe.

Evidence from indicator plants, therefore, should be based on a suite of species rather than a single one. Where possible it should be based on their behaviour in the same region, and not extrapolated from other parts of Britain. The method is likely to be more successful in areas where woods are few and well separated than in better-wooded districts.

The flora of recent woods consists mainly of plants that have no particular connection with woodland but are widespread in hedges and other habitats. Ivy, for instance, is very common in secondary woods, especially small ones, in many parts of the country, but it is uncommon in primary woods except round the edge. Ivy gets in in the early stages of forming a wood and may then last for centuries, but it does not readily colonize existing woodland and so it may mark out areas that have been added to a primary wood. Somewhat similar is cow-parsley (*Anthriscus sylvestris*), a very familiar plant of hedges, especially roadside hedges, and typical also of secondary woodland.

Management and the woodland flora

Management is nearly as important as continuity in determining the typical flora of ancient woodland. Management that involves long periods of continuous shade, combined with a heavy fall of tree leaves that do not easily rot, may produce a poor flora even in an ancient wood. Evergreen monocultures of conifers or rhododendrons are particularly unkind to the ground vegetation; hawthorn and sycamore are not much better.

In Sutton Coldfield Park a poor woodland flora is attributable partly to unfavourable dominant trees, continuous oak and holly. The beech woods on the acid soils of the Chiltern plateau are largely derived from prehistoric forest, often via a wood-pasture stage, but for some 200 years have been carefully managed as 'high forest' producing timber only. They now have a plantation-like appearance with miles of tall beeches, beautiful but monotonous, varied only by a few oaks and the occasional giant wild cherry. Ground vegetation is very sparse; underwood is almost non-existent, except around wood edges and near internal banks where there are hornbeam (probably originally planted to form a shade-bearing boundary hedge), whitebeam, etc. Immediately outside the woods are fields and lanes whose ancient hedges have a quite different and wider range of trees, shrubs, and other plants. Although the woods are sometimes on poorer soil the remarkably abrupt contrast between the plantation-like woods and the wood-like hedges must be mainly due to past management encouraging the densely shading beech.

Wild and planted trees

Planting covers a wide range of activities. At one extreme it may consist of burying acorns where they fall from the tree and thereby giving them a slightly better chance of establishment than they would have had if they remained on the surface. It is perhaps unimportant to distinguish a wood so treated from one managed by felling alone. At the other extreme 'planting' may consist of grubbing out a wood and growing spruce on the site. The archaeologist will be chiefly interested in those forms of planting which are not so gentle as to be insignificant, nor so drastic as to efface all the earlier vegetation.

Where woods contain non-naturalized trees such as horse-chestnut, Norway spruce, or 'commercial' poplars these have invariably been put there by the hand of man. The same applies to the common lime, except in rare cases of natural hybrids (page 37). It is more difficult to determine the planting of native trees such as oak and ash, or of naturalized species such as sweet-chestnut, sycamore, and (in Scotland) beech.

Oak, the most commonly planted native tree, consists of two species. Until very recent years the pedunculate oak was more favoured by planters, especially in Scotland, than the sessile. Of the two oaks the sessile is more strongly associated with ancient unplanted woodland; but it is unwise to suppose that pedunculate oak necessarily results from planting.

In regions such as East Anglia, where oak is nearly all pedunculate, the oaks of most ancient woods are nevertheless exceedingly variable. The trunk may be straight, curved, or corkscrew, smooth or burred; the branches and twigs may be spreading or erect; the foliage uniform or clustered; the leaves may fall as early as October or as late as January; and occasionally there are such bizarre features as bright scarlet shoots in August. Most of these variations appear to be due to heredity more than to the environment or age of the tree. Such irregular oak populations probably represent the natural variation of prehistoric oaks, maintained down the centuries by natural regeneration assisted, if at all, by planting from local stock which does not affect the genetic make-up of the population. Oaks obtained from nurseries, in contrast, tend to be all the same and to have been selected for modern ideas of timber quality. In a minority of ancient woods the oaks are clearly an intrusion from outside sources. They are all of the same age, often mid nineteenth century and all cast in the same genetic mould with straight trunks and few burrs. Often they are in regular rows and set so close together as to interfere seriously with the underwood or even with each other. Yet even in such woods one finds the occasional deviant tree, older than the others, that tells of a wild oak population that has not been entirely suppressed.

Similar variations can be used to distinguish 'wild' populations of other trees such as ash and hornbeam. Trees of wild origin, as in the Bradfield Woods or Hatfield Forest, often look quite different from the same species in plantations or arboreta.

Woodland elms

Elms (other than the wych-elm) are particularly interesting trees. They have been long and intimately associated with man, they are extremely variable, and, uniquely among cultivated plants, their variations are indefinitely perpetuated by suckering.

Elms in woods display a complex interaction between human activities, woodland ecology, and elm reproduction. There are six ways in which non-*glabra* elms could, in principle, get into woods:

1) By having been on the site ever since it was Wildwood. This is possible in some cases but most woodland elms can be explained in other ways.
2) By deliberate planting—probably rare.
3) By invasion of farmland (page 98)—many elm groves and belts have originated thus.
4) By invasion of existing woodland from an elm hedge.
5) By natural establishment from seed in an existing wood. This is a rare event because the weather and the state of the coppice both have to be favourable simultaneously; but it is important because it may give rise to new sorts of elm. Many small elm clones round wood edges started in this way.
6) By suckering from elms originally planted round a settlement.

When looking at a wood in detail one can learn much about its history by mapping the elms, deciding where each clone came from, how rapidly it is invading, and whether there are any remains of trees that grew on the site before the elms. Perhaps the most interesting are the settlement elms, especially in East Anglia and Cornwall where elms are both common and variable, because they give us our one opportunity of direct contact with the varieties of plants that grew around settlements that are now deserted.

The meaning of stinging-nettles

The stinging-nettle is one of a group of plants that indicate unusually fertile soil; others are elderberry and goose-grass (*Galium aparine*). Nettles are greedy for phosphate, and their roots are inefficient at getting it.[63] Some soils are naturally rich in phosphate; but most ancient woods are on soils too poor to support nettles, which therefore generally indicate places where phosphate has been artificially accumulated.

Man is a phosphate-gathering animal. All crops contain phosphorus; every consumer of wheat, faggots or sheep is transporting phosphate from the countryside at large into built-up areas. Little of this ever goes back whence it came. Phosphate accumulates particularly in bones and ashes. Most of it goes to feed the nettles in gardens and on rubbish-tips, while some of it awaits the Last Trump in country churchyards. Especially in alkaline soils, phosphate is extremely persistent in the ground, which is why deserted gardens, rubbish-tips, and churchyards often remain nettle-grown for centuries. In Overhall Grove, Boxworth, Cambridgeshire, the phosphate accumulated by the high living of the Hobridges still gives rise to several acres of ear-high nettles around the site of their manor-house, deserted for at least 400 years. Nettles do not necessarily indicate secondary woodland; countrymen have long been in the habit of throwing their rubbish into the nearest grove, and sufficient phosphate may be accumulated by bonfires or by a big roost of starlings. Nevertheless the investigator should not pass an area of nettles in an otherwise nettle-free wood without considering the possibility that the site has been inhabited.

Buff Wood, East Hatley, Cambridgeshire

Two examples will illustrate the way in which the evidence of documents, earthworks, flora and vegetation can be made to complement each other in making a historical synthesis.

Buff Wood (Fig. 21) overlies part of the shrunken village of East Hatley, and its complicated earthworks include two moats and four areas of ridge-and-furrow. Written evidence indicates that the wood has covered virtually the same area since before 1650. There is a nucleus that may well be primary woodland. This has boundary banks but no internal earthworks; it is an ash-maple-hazel coppice with aspens and standard oak trees, very like the medieval Hayley Wood near by; it has oxlip, mercury, woodland hawthorn, and a wealth of other plants; and it apparently coincides with a wood specified in the Hundred Rolls of 1279.

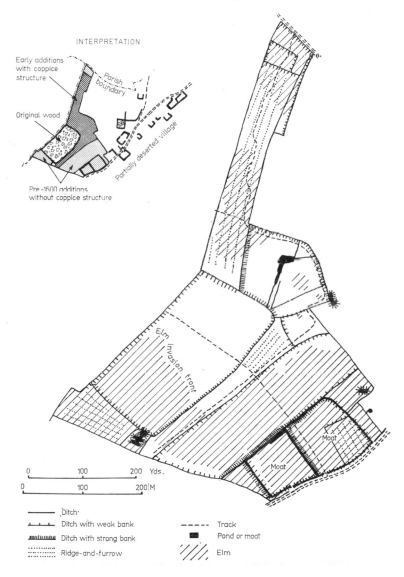

INTERPRETATION

Early additions
with coppice
structure

Parish boundary

Original wood

Partially deserted village

Pre-1600 additions
without coppice structure

Elm invasion front

Moat

Moat

0   100   200 Yds.

0   100   200 M

——— Ditch
⊥⊥⊥ Ditch with weak bank
▬▬▬ Ditch with strong bank
∷∷∷ Ridge-and-furrow

- - - - Track
■ Pond or moat
///, Elm

Fig. 21. Buff Wood in East Hatley, Cambridgeshire.

The secondary woodland areas nearest the original wood are virtually indistinguishable from it in their vegetation, as we might expect after at least 300 years of direct contact. They too have ash and maple stools, some of them very large. They do, however, have ivy and spurge-laurel (a secondary woodland indicator in this district). The secondary woodland towards the moats has no coppice structure and there is no sign that it has ever been dominated by anything other than elm.

Elms are an outstanding feature of Buff Wood. At least 29 clones are involved; most of them are visibly distinct from each other, and between them they cover much of the total variation of British elms. Different elms have got into the wood by succession, invasion from hedges, seed, and planting; with varying degrees of vigour they have invaded the secondary woodland and much of the original wood, and they impinge on one another in different ways. The biggest concentration of elms is in the area of the old village; within the two moats there are no less than 10 different elm clones, some of which appear to occupy specific positions as though directly descended from elm hedges planted by the moat-dwellers. The whole of one moat and part of the other are occupied by vigorous nettle-beds.

The later history of Buff Wood involved some localized tree-planting: a few rows of oak and hybrid poplar, the odd common lime and Huntingdon elm, while some unsuccessful beech, larch, and spruce still soldier on as witnesses to the boundless optimism of the Victorian forester. The last addition to Buff Wood was in the 1860s, and until recent years one could see there one primrose-cowslip hybrid plant, a vestige of the previous pasture. Coppicing, which had lapsed around 1910, was resumed by Cambridge University in 1955, and Buff is now one of the most instructive and colourful of woods.

Groton Wood, West Suffolk

This wood, now the property of the Suffolk Trust for Nature Conservation, is a soil on which neither oxlip nor ridge-and-furrow occurs. It falls into two parts (Fig. 22). The northern third is surrounded by a massive, sinuous, and partly double earthwork of early wood-bank type, except on the north where

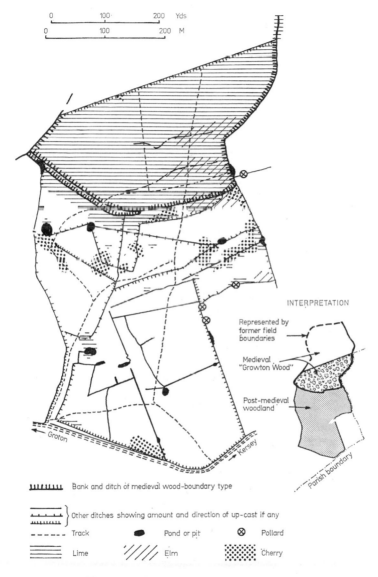

0   100   200   Yds
0   100   200   M

INTERPRETATION

Represented by
former field
boundaries

Medieval
"Growton Wood"

Post-medieval
woodland

Parish boundary

Groton

Kersey

⊔⊔⊔⊔⊔⊔⊔   Bank and ditch of medieval wood-boundary type

Other ditches showing amount and direction of up-cast if any

- - - - - -   Track   ⬤   Pond or pit   ⊗   Pollard

═══   Lime   /////   Elm   ▦   Cherry

Fig. 22.   Groton Wood, W. Suffolk.

there is a straight and much less substantial boundary. Its only internal features are two faint streams. The southern two-thirds has only slight boundary earthworks, but is criss-crossed with a tangle of low banks and ditches and contains numerous pits and ponds.

The earthworks show that the present outline of Groton Wood, although known to date from before 1778, cannot be its original shape. The original wood is undoubtedly the northern part, which has been truncated on its north side and enlarged on the south, where some of the earthworks probably represent the hedge-banks of former fields. This is abundantly confirmed by the vegetation. The northern wood is dominated by huge stools of small-leaved lime, accompanied in wet hollows by elm (not an invasive elm, but one of the coppicing sorts that sometimes go with lime in Suffolk and may have done so since before the Elm Decline). The southern part has small, irregular, scattered coppice stools of ash, hazel, etc., and also has many trees of the wild cherry. Lime is strongly associated with primary woodland, while cherry, in this area, is nearly as good an indicator of secondary woodland and wood margins.

Indirect references to lime in Groton go back to 1279. The 'Growton wood' of 37 acres, confiscated from Bury St Edmunds Abbey and bestowed by Henry VIII on Adam Winthrop I, fits very well with the present northern wood plus two 'Wood Fields' to the north which are bounded by a sinuous hedge consisting, in part, of massive lime stools. The alterations to the wood therefore probably took place between 1544 and 1778. One is tempted to attribute the enlargement to John Winthrop II, who sold Groton Wood when in 1631 he went off to found the State of Massachusetts, and who had previously been the co-author of a pamphlet advocating woodland conservation.[64]

It is notable that the boundary of the lime does not quite coincide with the old wood-bank but overlaps it by a few yards. Elsewhere in the southern wood there are occasional lime stools, often on banks. Lime must have been given an exceptionally good opportunity for colonization when the new wood was being formed adjacent to an existing lime grove. Yet, even so, few trees became established more than 25 yards outside the old boundary, and some of those may already have been there in the field hedges.

7 Trees on commons: the wood-pasture tradition

By Langley Bush I roam but the bush hath left its hill
On Cowper Green I stray tis a desert strange and chill
And spreading Lea Close Oak ere decay had penned its will
To the axe of the spoiler and self interest fell a prey
And Crossberry Way and old Round Oaks narrow Lane
With its hollow trees like pulpits I shall never see again
Inclosure like a Buonaparte let not a thing remain
It levelled every bush and tree and levelled every hill . . .
John Clare, *Remembrances* [the Inclosure is that
of Helpston, Peterborough, in 1809]

The practice of using the same piece of land for trees and agriculture presumably goes back to prehistoric times, and is well documented from the early Middle Ages. While woodland itself may involve some conflict of interest, if only between timber and underwood, the conflict between the two elements in wood-pasture is more severe. The more trees there are, the less abundant and the worse will be the pasture, and the more animals graze the pasture, the more difficult it becomes to replace the trees. This conflict has been resolved, or stabilized, in four different sets of ways on commons, in parks, Forests, and in hedges.

By the thirteenth century much of the Domesday Book wood-pasture had disappeared. Eastern England had little left except in the Royal Forests, although it was still extensive in some other areas. As late as 1305, a tenant of Great Horwood, Buckinghamshire, accused of not ploughing his lord's land as he was obliged to do under the terms of his tenancy, was able to get away with the excuse that his plough-oxen were grazing in the manor woods, and he needed three days' notice to round them up.[65] The decline of wood-pasture is partly due to conversion to other land uses.

Conversion to parks or coppice woods is less well documented than asserting for agriculture, although in cases such as Shipdham, Norfolk, where a large Domesday pannage record coincides with a large thirteenth-century coppice wood it is probable that the wood was converted to coppicing before its structure had been too far damaged by grazing. Similar encoppicements took place sporadically throughout the historical period, and some well-known woods, such as Wytham Woods near Oxford and The Mens, W. Sussex, have a common-land history.

In many cases an early wood-pasture turned into a treeless common because the pasture element gained the upper hand and grazing was sufficient to prevent the replacement of the trees. In the case of Thorpe Wood, Norwich, enough twelfth-century documents survive for us to establish what happened to a Domesday pannage wood, a story which is undoubtedly typical of the rise and decline of many commons.

Domesday Book says that Thorpe had a wood 'for 1200 swine', one of the largest assessments in Norfolk. Thorpe Wood was bestowed on the bishopric of Norwich by Henry I in 1101. From topographical allusions in contemporary discussions of the bizarre and sinister affair of 'St William of Norwich' we learn that in the 1140s Thorpe Wood occupied the whole of the present Mousehold Heath as well as its later site on the steep slopes above the river (Fig. 23).[66] Herbert de Losinga, first bishop of Norwich, wrote a letter to his woodward which provides the earliest record of an interest in woodland conservation on the part of an individual:

> As to making a present of Thorpe Wood to the sick or anyone else, I gave you no orders, nor did I give nor will I give any; for I appointed you the custodian of the Wood, not the rooter up of it. To the sick, when I come to Norwich, I will give as I did last year, not logs of wood, but money. . . . Guard the Wood of the Holy Trinity, as you wish to be guarded by the Holy Trinity, and to continue in my favour.

Probably Thorpe Wood was subject to grazing rights over which the bishop had no control. The development of Mousehold Heath, which he evidently anticipated and tried to postpone, is first recorded in 1156 by Pope Adrian IV, who refers to 'the

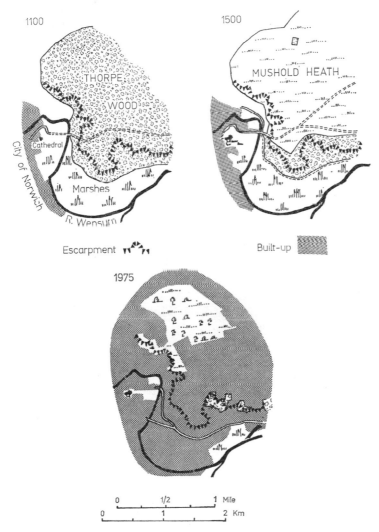

Fig. 23. Development of Mousehold (Mushold) Heath, Norwich.

Heath with all its wood'.[67] By 1236 we find a reference to 'the part of Thorpe Wood which was covered with oaks' in contrast to the heath part of the wood. Late medieval perambulations and sixteenth-century maps and views depict a new state of stability with managed woodland on the southern slopes, while the gravelly plateau was heathland with common rights for sheep, cattle, and pigs. Wood-consuming installations nearby included the bishop's lime-kiln and the Lollards' Pit, 'where men are customablie burnt'.

Both the wood and the heath have since been eaten away by enclosure-act farmers and speculative builders. The Wood of the Holy Trinity is now reduced to steep fragments, drastically planted with exotic trees, in which a few pollard oaks, ancient beeches, and the occasional stool of small-leaved lime linger on. Mousehold Heath, like many English commons, now suffers from lack of grazing, lack of rabbits, and the efficiency of the Fire Brigade; most of the once glorious heathland has turned into secondary oak and birch woodland.

Although wood-pasture systems are less stable ecologically and socially than coppice, not all commons lost their trees in this way. At Minchinhampton, Gloucestershire, for instance, there were some 2,000 acres of woods, some of them privately owned but all subject to various common rights both of wood and pasture. The woods were jealously protected by the medieval courts of the manor against over-exploitation by any of their users. They were still in a flourishing state in 1538 and most of them were still there when the system finally broke down in the seventeenth century.[68] Even without such regulation, grazing was not always sufficiently intensive or continuous to prevent the trees from regenerating. When grazing declined, as on many commons nowadays, trees could increase. Commons that were normally woodless sometimes grew scrub—at Little Gransden, Cambridgeshire, the sixteenth-century villagers cut 'busshes and trees of about the bignes of a mans legge' on Langland Common (Rackham 1975); Burnham Beeches, Buckinghamshire, appears to have arisen in the seventeenth century on common land with few trees.[69]

Although coppice was sometimes possible where the pasture element was slight, the tree form best adapted to commons as to other kinds of wood-pasture is the pollard. Pollard trees produced wood on a continuous basis, which went to the villagers or to their lord according to local custom.

Commons are the least well preserved of all types of tree-land. They were a particular target of the enclosure movement, especially the larger and less intensively grazed commons which were the ones that most often had trees. Once a common was enclosed it was usually destroyed, although there are exceptions, as with parts of Little Baddow Common, Essex, where the oak coppice stools and pollards still stand because the soil is too poor to repay grubbing them out. Even where a common survives, its historic features are often obscured by secondary woodland.

Commons, both wooded and unwooded, have a distinctive shape which is quite different from the shape of woods. They have a straggling concave outline (Fig. 24) tapering away gradually into the roads which cross the common. Commons are surrounded by houses which front on to the common and back on to their own private land. A typical unit of settlement in the Ancient Countryside, particularly of East Anglia, is the green or 'tye' of an acre or two, with two or three cottages, at the junction of three or four roads. Greens come in all sizes above this; often they are interconnected, as in the magnificent series of greens, much of which still remains, rambling across six parishes around Long Stratton, Norfolk. There is a continuous range of sizes up to Epping Forest, which in social terms is the largest green of all. Chapman and André's map of Essex in 1777 (which, like other early county maps, is more detailed and reliable for common land than for woods) shows the Forest relatively unaffected by modern development, with its concave straggling outline and hundreds of boundary houses.

The boundaries of wooded commons usually have a slight and not very distinctive bank and ditch. Where a common abuts on a wood the latter has a normal wood-bank (Plate x).

Despite these differences of shape, ancient woods and some greens have a common origin in remnants of Wildwood. The wooded commons of Middlesex continued a strong wood-pasture tradition in that county going back to the very large pannage entries for several parishes in Domesday Book. Around Fressingfield, Suffolk, which has long been a very woodless area, the numerous Domesday pannage woods appear to have turned into large greens, some with wood-names like Greshaw and Alwood Green. However, most greens already existed in the early Middle Ages and the circumstances of their origin are not recorded. It is hard to believe that they all started in this way or

139

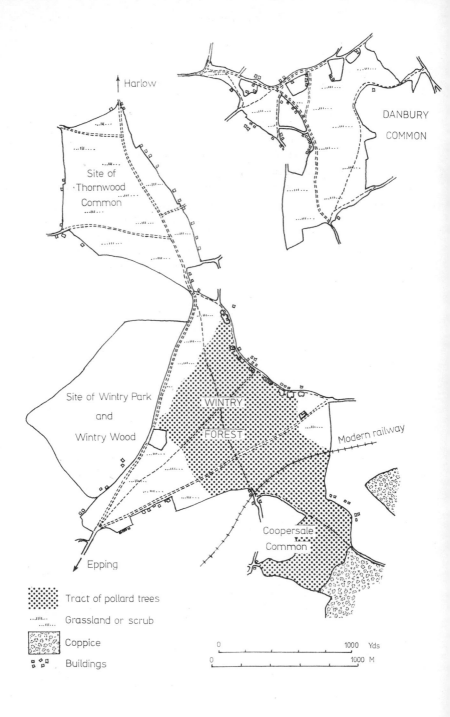

↑ Harlow

DANBURY
COMMON

Site of
Thornwood
Common

Site of Wintry Park

and

Wintry Wood

WINTRY

FOREST

Modern railway

Coopersale
Common

↓ Epping

Tract of pollard trees

Grassland or scrub

Coppice

Buildings

0   1000   Yds

0   1000   M

that every little tye, with the lanes leading to it, represents a grove.

Even where a wooded common is on the site of a Wildwood remnant it does not follow that it is primary woodland in the sense that we have seen for coppice woods. Continuity of vegetation is more difficult to establish for wood-pasture. If a wood loses its trees it ceases to be a wood and disappears from the record. A common is more likely to lose its trees and, if it does so, does not cease to be a common; if grazing later relaxes, the trees may unobtrusively return.

The majority of woodland on commons is less than a century old. Embedded in it there may sometimes be pollards, usually of oak, beech (Plate VIII), or hornbeam. Ancient trees of other species are less frequent. Elms, for instance, are abundant in the field hedges around Essex and Middlesex commons, and fringe the boundaries of commons, but are rare in commons themselves—a striking instance of the effect of different management systems on tree species. Coopersale Common, Essex (Fig. 24), is a remarkable instance where management for underwood appears to have gained the upper hand quite recently: it has a dense dark stand of innumerable small hornbeam pollards which must have been cut within the last thirty years.

The ground vegetation of wooded commons seldom contains any of the more exacting woodland plants of the district, except where they have survived in odd corners (for example, along streams) and have later been able to recolonize. As a possible compensation, the ancient trees provide habitats for the more exacting lichens and invertebrate animals (page 150), although many of the best commons, alas, are in places now too air-polluted for lichens.

Fig. 24. Shapes of commons.
Danbury Common, Essex. Medium-sized common with straggling concave outline, crossed by roads and tracks, and with houses around margin and in enclaves. No surviving wood (although much recent secondary woodland). Wintry Forest and associated commons near Epping, Essex. Large interconnected commons with tracts of pollard trees. Demarcated from adjoining woods and park but not from roads. Note shape and boundary houses. (Shown as in 1874 before suburban encroachment.)

8 Parks: private wood-pasture

The same Manor of Redgrave is A manor within whiche . . .
there is A park wt dere in the same . . . the herbage
of the parke there is not above valued. . . .
Lytel Coppies nyghe the parke conteyneth 15 acres.
Freyth Coppies conteyneth 44 acres.
Redgrave Wood conteyneth 45 acres.
In the parke be 30 acres thyn sett with pollyng * okes
and hardebeme † growing by parcelles. . . .
[Detailed census of the coppices follows.]
The sprynge ‡ . . . of 30 acres not valuyd because the wood ys old . . .
which once fallen shall never be any wood agayne.

*Valuation of part of the Suffolk estates of
Bury St Edmunds Abbey, c. 1540* 7⁰

The word *park* has meant many things down the centuries.
The Anglo-Saxon *pearroc* meant any piece of land with a fence
round it. Later it was a place for keeping deer; then the outer
and less formal part of the grounds around a gentleman's house;
and nowadays it is where one airs the dog amid geraniums and
begonias. These meanings are not as distinct in practice as one
might expect. Even the earliest meaning survives in Cornish and
Welsh place-names. The landscape and recreation aspects of
parks already existed, at least in embryo, in the Middle Ages, and
several medieval parks have turned into town gardens.

The deer-park tradition

The classical meaning of *park* in England and Wales is an enclosure for semi-wild animals. By far the commonest beast of the
park was the fallow deer, the introduction of which, probably by

---

* Pollard.   † Hornbeam.   ‡ Regrowth.

William the Conqueror, was an important factor in perpetuating the wood-pasture tradition. There are some supposed archaeological or documentary records of fallow deer in Britain before the Conquest, but Dr D. Chapman tells me that none of these has withstood critical examination. This animal rapidly increased to become the most important beast of the medieval chase. At that time, and for long after, it was confined to parks or concentrated in Royal Forests and did not roam the countryside as it does now. Its introduction appears to have been a semi-agricultural enterprise, a new means of exploiting land, comparable to the cattle ranches of the American Mid-West. Some parks contained (as a few still do) red deer or semi-wild white cattle; we also hear of hare parks and swine-parks (for wild boar, a rare curiosity by the late Middle Ages). On the Earl's Colne Map of 1598 (frontispiece) Chalkney Wood bears the inscription: 'Chawlkny woodd In wch woodd the Erles of Oxenforde in tymes paste bredd and mayntayned wyelde Swyne And in the reigne of kinge Henry the eight John then Erle of Oxenforde caused them to be destroied for the greate damage and hurte the Contrie susteined by them'.

The Anglo-Saxons, having no fallow deer, had—as far as we know—no Royal Forests and not many parks. Among the few parks in Domesday Book is the 'park of woodland beasts' at Borough Green, Cambridgeshire, the remains of whose massive earthworks still exist in Burrough-Green Park Wood. Other very early parks are those like Barnsdale Park, Rutland (Fig. 25), and Ongar Park, Essex, which are older than the parish boundary system, since the parish boundaries deviate to follow the park outline. By the thirteenth century there were many parks; from then on a licensing procedure was introduced which gives us a systematic record of their formation.

Medieval parks have been listed in some counties. Mr W. Liddell and Mr J. Hunter have found 103 pre-1536 parks in Essex and Mr P. Nicholson 18–22 in E. Suffolk; C. C. Taylor[10] gives 90 for Dorset. These figures are inevitably incomplete, and not all these parks existed simultaneously. Nevertheless if these counties are representative of lowland England, parks in their heyday around 1330 must have been more prominent in the landscape than at any later period, with roughly 1 park to every 4 parishes or to every 15 square miles.

The deer of Forests were at liberty to stray on to surrounding land, but those of parks were confined by a deer-proof boundary, the upkeep of which dominated park economics, since fallow deer are as strong as pigs and more agile than goats. The characteristic boundary was the park pale, a special palisade of cleft-oak stakes, whose maintenance was very expensive in labour and in high-quality timber. An alternative to the park pale might be a

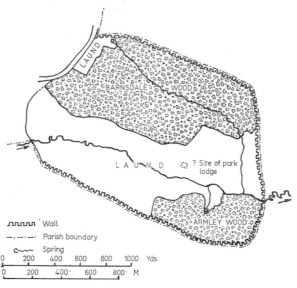

Fig. 25. Barnsdale Park, Rutland. Large early deer park (first heard of in 1269) with 'economical' outline, woods, launds, and site of lodge. Shown as in 1850.

wall, as in the great East Midland parks—Barnsdale, Burley, Burghley—which are just outside stone-wall country. We also hear of park hedges.

The earliest parks have a characteristic compact outline with rounded corners (Fig. 25) which suggests economy in fencing. Later medieval parks were often small or awkwardly shaped, perhaps because of difficulties in acquiring the land, and some of them were short-lived. The bigger the park, the less boundary it has in relation to its area, and the cheaper it is to fence per acre enclosed. Yet we often hear of parks of 30 acres or less, which must have been well below the viable minimum. A park was the rich man's privilege—a valuable one, since it kept him in fresh meat over the winter—and the not-quite-so-rich man's status symbol. Parks could vary enormously in appearance and were no exception to the general medieval practice of multiple uses for the same piece of land. Some of these land uses might remain from the previous history of the site, for it was seldom possible to find a completely vacant piece of land to empark. Most parks contained considerable areas of woodland or trees, but the proportions could vary widely. The 'parkland' combination of grassland and scattered, often pollarded, trees was common but not universal.

Many small parks were formed by emparking the whole of an existing wood; at the other extreme we occasionally hear of treeless parks. Other land uses included pasture for cattle and sheep and sometimes even arable, meadow and common grazing. The existence of all these conflicting activities implies that deer were not always in practice the predominant objective of park management that they were in theory.

The Ely Coucher Book of 1251, in surveying the Pulhams, S. Norfolk, states:

The wood
Item there is one park which contains in all sixty acres by estimate, part of which is 29½ acres of arable land in the launds of the same park which are included in the total of arable land . . . the pasture is worth 10*d*. per acre.

Item there is a wood called grischaue [later Greshaw Wood, now vanished] which contains 100 acres by estimate . . . from which the underwood of 25 acres together with the herbage are worth 40*s*. per annum.
[Two small groves follow.]

The Coucher Book refers to many other parks, one of which, at Barking, Suffolk, is described on page 66.

In 1386 Abbot Tymworth's survey [71] of the great estate of Long Melford, W. Suffolk (Fig. 15), includes:

Woods
In the great wood 260 acres by estimate, in which can be made every year 600 faggots, worth 8*s*. (at 16*d*. the hundred). The agistment in the same is worth £2 per annum.

In the wood called lenyng 90 acres, one-sixth part of which each year is 15 acres which are worth £2 12s. 6d. at 3s. 6d. per acre.

Le Speltne is 80 acres by estimate, one-sixth part of which each year is worth £2 7s. 10d. at 3s. 6d. per acre.

In the little park 60 acres and the wood is worth £1 10s. per annum at 3s. per acre. [*sic*]

Cutting thorns in various places is worth 12d. a year.

Pannage of pigs worth 6s. 8d. a year.

Total £9 6s. 0d. a year.

Under the heading of pasture is included 5 acres 'in the little park in the laund' which brought in 2s. 6d. per annum.

Long Melford Great Wood was certainly a park; earlier and later documents call it Elmsett Park. Its site is occupied by a modern Park Farm. Lenyng and le Speltne are Lineage and Spelthorne Woods, which survived in their medieval form until the 1960s (Fig. 15). The Little Park was later superseded by the present Melford Park. Agistment is the letting of grazing land by the year to outside farmers.

As these surveys illustrate, parks and woods were associated in the medieval mind but were not identical in practice. At Long Melford one-sixth of each of the *woods* was supposed to be felled each year on a coppice rotation. Elmsett *Park*, although called the Great Wood, produced much less income in proportion to its size, and most of this was from 'agistment'. It produced only a trivial amount of wood each year, which was expressed not in terms of acres of underwood, implying the felling of blocks of continuous coppice, but as hundreds of faggots, which must have come from the pollarding of sparsely scattered trees. The Little Park, in contrast, was mainly woodland, felled on a six-year rotation like the other woods, although evidently of slightly lower quality; it also contained a defined tract of pasture called a *laund*; this word—probably related to the 'lawns' in Forests—is commonly used for treeless areas within parks.

The Ely Coucher Book surveys, although less detailed, illustrate the fact that this variety of arrangements existed already in the thirteenth century. The parks at Pulham and Barking included launds; the laund at Pulham was actually under the plough, and since arable farming must have been totally incompatible with deer on so small an area as 60 acres there can hardly have been any deer in the park at the time. Even so, the return from the 'wood' part of the park is in the form of pasture, which implies a parkland type of vegetation. Greshaw *Wood*, in contrast, although much larger, was intensively managed as woodland on the four-year coppice cycle which was common at the time.

Deer, even in moderate numbers, are not compatible with normal woodland management because they eat young under-wood and seedling trees. Every owner of a woodland deer park must eventually have been faced with three options for its future. He could give up the deer and allow the park to continue as coppice wood; this was the most likely course of events in small woodland parks, which would be difficult to maintain because of the expense of fencing. At Barking the tiny park of 1251 survives (Fig. 11) as one of the many small Park Woods in which only the name remains as a record of a brief attempt to set up a deer park. The second option was to give up the underwood and retain only scattered long-lived trees, pollards and big timber. Pulham Park probably became parkland, that is trees plus grass, before 1251. At Long Melford, Elmsett Park had diverged from the main stream of woodland management before 1386, while Little Park became parkland by 1580.

The third option of a park owner was to combine his deer and his wood: to divide his park into compartments, some of which were grassland (with or without trees) and some woodland. The wooded compartments could be fenced for the first few years after felling, until the underwood had grown big enough for the deer not to harm it seriously. The launds provided grass for the deer and places where they could be hunted for sport. Launds, as we have seen, were a common adjunct even to a small park, but the system would only work well in the bigger parks. Barnsdale Park (Fig. 25) showed, until recently altered by replanting and the Empingham Reservoir, a probably typical arrangement of woods around a central clearing. The earthworks around smaller launds are shown in Fig. 14. A particularly grand example is Sutton Coldfield Park, surviving miraculously in the midst of the Birmingham conurbation, with its enclosed 'hursts'—embanked

woods, formerly coppiced—around a great open plain of grassland and heath which ramifies between the hursts. It is similar in
scale to the smaller Forests such as Hatfield Forest, Essex,
although it differs in its compact park-like outer perimeter.

Besides pollards, the open parts of medieval parks contained
timber trees, mainly oak, which were allowed to grow bigger
than those in woods—a wise treatment since it was more difficult
to replace them. As early as 1274 royal officials came to Stansted
Mountfitchet and confiscated 80 oaks valued at 4*d*. each from
Hasishey (now Alsa) Wood, while the trees that they took from a
nearby park were worth six times as much each.[72] Parks provided
many of the outsize trees for structures such as King's College
Chapel, Cambridge, and, in a later period, the large or specially
shaped timbers used by shipbuilders (Rackham 1974).

The landscape-park tradition

The educated public is brought up to regard parks, like other
features of the British countryside, as an essentially eighteenth-
century invention. By discussing medieval parks at some length
I have tried to restore the balance. The history of eighteenth-
century parks has been extensively studied, since they were the
work of a comparatively small number of well-known designers
and schools of landscape design. The reader is referred to Prince
(1958) and Hadfield (1967).

The medieval park was a mainly utilitarian enterprise, a special
kind of farm producing venison. Many parks, including most of
those so far named, were a long way from the owner's house;
the park business was carried on from a lodge in the middle of the
park. However, some medieval parks, from Windsor Great Park
downwards, provided a worthy setting for lordly or monkish
mansions. Even the remoter parks already had their aspects of
pleasure and romance. The terse words of the chronicler do not
altogether conceal the pride and joy of the monks of Butley, Suffolk,
when in 1528 they took the Queen of France for a picnic 'under
the oaks' of their newly acquired Staverton Park (Peterken 1969).

The post-medieval history of parks was more of a continuous
process than is often supposed. Many medieval deer parks were
given a new lease of life as landscape parks. Most of the stock-in-

trade both of the seventeenth- and of the eighteenth-century landscape designer consisted of elements from the medieval countryside; in many cases existing features were adapted. Avenues would occur naturally to anyone familiar with hedgerow trees along a road. Ornamental lakes, where not adapted from existing fishponds, may have been modelled on medieval industrial reservoirs such as those in Sutton Coldfield Park. The Long Melford map of 1613 shows a new park, very like those engraved by Kip (*fl.* 1690–1720) a century later; there is a parallel map of 1580 which shows that its groves were formed, in part, by dissecting a wood, its big trees were there in a meadow, and its lines of trees were formed by hedgerow trees from which the hedge had been removed.

Lancelot Brown (1716–1783), the greatest of landscape designers, was widely celebrated and criticized by his contemporaries as a destroyer of existing features and creator of new ones. It is easy to suppose a 'Capability Brown' park to be entirely Brown's creation, and even to credit the master with transforming wide tracts of countryside. But we must distinguish between landscape gardens and landscape parks. The influence of Brown and his successors on the former was much more revolutionary—in physical terms—than on the latter. Gardens are small and relatively formal areas which can easily be transformed, and have been transformed so often that pre-Brown examples seldom survive. With parks the scale of operations was much larger and the transformations slower and more expensive, and in consequence 'landscaping' involved *leaving* trees as well as *planting* them. Sometimes, as at Audley End, Essex, we have a new Brown park in which no earlier trees remain. But a large proportion of Brown's prolific output involved limited alterations to existing parks: removing an avenue, adding a lake here, a grove there, and a belt of trees round the boundary. At Heveningham, Suffolk, for instance, Brown's 'before and after' drawings show that he recorded and preserved many pollards and thorn bushes, some of which are still there. Repton, Brown's more conservative successor, shows in his writings that he appreciated and preserved the beauty of ancient trees; his fold-out pictures demonstrate his skill in achieving picturesque effects by means of small but judicious physical changes.

149

Parks as they are now

Occasionally a medieval park survives in working order. At Moccas, Herefordshire, the fallow deer, cattle, and sheep share the grass beneath oaks and ashes whose slow growth sees the centuries slip by, and which in their bizarre shapes, textures, and colours express the strange beauty of extremely aged trees (Plate xi). This Arcadian scene is completed by the cleft-oak park pale and the brackeny mountain behind. In other cases, through a historical accident, a complete park may survive out of use, as with Sutton Coldfield and its woods, or Staverton and its pollards. The majority of medieval parks survive either in later parks or as fragments: a few pollard trees, a boundary earthwork, a boundary hedge (as at Hatfield Broadoak), a significant bend in a parish boundary, a 'Park Wood', or a mere name such as Park Farm or Lodge Farm.

Where an ancient park is still a park it is often possible to sort out the stages in its development, and to discern the trees and other features of the original deer park behind the overlay of the landscaping period, the Victorian conifers and pheasant coverts, and in some cases (for example, Christchurch Park, Ipswich) recent municipalization.

Although pollard trees are a frequent and characteristic feature of ancient parks, as far as I know none of them are still pollarded: in most cases they have not been cut for 200 years or more.

Park boundary earthworks are of various types: some medieval parks have a bank with *internal* ditch (page 115).

Parks, like commons, seldom have many of the flowering-plants characteristic of ancient woodland, and for the same reason. The native trees of parks are likewise more limited than in woods, though one occasionally finds the more exacting species such as small-leaved lime. However, ancient parks excel in lichens and in the invertebrate fauna of dead wood. Dr Francis Rose has listed (1974) 49 species of lichens (plus 8 mosses and liverworts) which grow on old trees and are correlated with ancient wood-pasture in the same way as some flowering-plants are indicators of ancient coppice woods. Many of Dr Rose's best sites, including the supremely rich Boconnoc, Cornwall, are parks. These species appear to be derived from the Wildwood; they grow only on very old dry bark with plenty of light and little disturbance, an environment which seldom occurs in woods but is provided by parkland.

Parks of the sixteenth and seventeenth centuries seldom survive in anything like their original form. A fine example is the Cambridge Backs, the predecessors of whose avenues, groves, tree-lined meadows, and various sorts of gardens are shown in part on Hamond's town-plan of 1592.

Occasionally the actual trees of an early avenue survive. The 300-odd trees of the lime avenue of Kentwell Hall in Long Melford date from about 1678 (the written evidence is confirmed by a ring-count), just before the main period of popularity of the common lime. They, too, appear to be a hybrid between *Tilia cordata* and *T. platyphyllos*, but they combine the features of these trees in a different (and more attractive) way from most forms of the common lime, and are possibly of local origin. The trees appear originally to have been pleached as a very formal avenue, but have now developed an immense height and spread. These limes have a distinctive habit of growth, reinforced by the pollard-like effect of their early pleaching and by the strange galls produced by generations of mistletoe. This venerable avenue is one of the more memorable features of a parish that is full of field antiquities.

9 Forests and chases: the king's wood-pasture

We find the said Forest ... to consist of Wood ground and Plains (that is to say) in Woodground usually incopsed and inclosed 646 Acres, in open Wood and Bushie ground 109 Acres, and in Playnes, Ridings and highways 240 Acres. The Forest appears irregular, full of angles and narrow Passages which wee conceive to be dangerous for the safetie of the Game of Deer there. ... By reason of the ... small Quantity of Playnes, the multitude of Sheep and other Cattle that depasture there (by pretence of Commonage) ... the Deere are forced to stray abroad for their Food. ... We find little Timber in the Forest worthy valuation. The open Woods consisting of Pollard Ash and Maple of small worth. ...

Royal Commission on Hatfield Forest, Essex, 1639 73

The mysterious word *forest* arose in the dark centuries after the fall of Rome, and got into most West European languages, in which it means either 1) a tract of land subject to special laws, usually concerned with the preservation of game, or 2) a tract of land covered with trees. It is not difficult to invent etymologies to support either meaning, and where learned philologists fail to agree a botanist shall not presume to decide which has priority.

Forests are first heard of in Britain in Domesday Book, where the word certainly has the first type of meaning. The Anglo-Saxon kings must have known of Continental Forest laws but themselves went little beyond the ordinary sporting rights of any landowner; the attribution of Forest law to Canute is a medieval forgery.74 Domesday records Forests in many areas, but casually and probably incompletely, and in terms which imply that the system was a recent development by the Conqueror.

Forests are well documented in easily accessible records and more has been published on their history than on that of any other ancient tree-land. For many counties an account will be found under 'Forestry' in the *Victoria County History*; more recent substantial accounts include those by C. E. Hart on the Forest of Dean (1966), by C. Tubbs on the New Forest (1968), and by Lord Ailesbury on Savernake (1962). Besides all these scholarly studies, some of whch are short on field-work, there have been many others bedevilled by popular mythology, by confusion of Royal Forests with woods or with modern forestry, and by excessive attention to Manwood's *Laws of the Forest* which, although quite a learned book, was written in 1598 and knows little of the practical operation of the Forests in earlier centuries.

Forests as institutions

The word Forest was a purely legal term—a tract of land where certain laws operated, as in our National Parks. The boundaries were not marked on the ground, and within them was a complete range of land uses including extensive arable and even towns like Colchester. Land could be afforested or disafforested by a stroke of the pen without any direct effect on the terrain. In addition to Royal Forests, there were others where similar by-laws operated in favour of magnates other than the king. Theoretically the word 'Forest' should be limited to Royal Forests, private ones being called 'chases', but there are many exceptions to this rule. At their greatest extent, Forests and chases covered about a fifth of England. The system was also imposed on Wales and there were analogous Forests in Scotland, but only in England did Forests have a strong influence on the landscape. To some extent their sites seem to us to have been chosen at random—they included whole counties, even civilized ones like Cornwall and Essex—but they tended to be based on big estates owned by the Crown and to include well-wooded or mountainous areas.

Every schoolboy is taught that Forests existed to provide deer and other game for the king's hunting, that all Plantagenet kings rode to hounds, like Jorrocks, four days a week, and the royal keepers roamed the land inflicting capital and surgical penalties on any peasant caught doing anything that might, however remotely, interfere with the deer. This idealistic picture has never been confirmed by critical research. Although it was a common reproach for an unpopular sovereign, like Edward II, that he spent too much time in the field, Forest records contain surprisingly few references to royal hunts. Hunting as a sport was an important, if sporadic, use of the Forests up to the Commonwealth, but we should look further to discover their main functions.

Dr Clifford Owen has shown, in his very illuminating researches, that the Forests were originally a royal business and not merely a hobby. The early-medieval kings and their courts lived largely on venison, and were prepared to devote much of their territory to producing it. The growth of the 'civil service', under the inexorable pressure of Parkinson's Law, was matched by a growth in the extent and bureaucracy of the Forests up to the time of King John. Kings after 1216 could no longer withstand the antagonism which Forests and their officials created among their subjects. The court ceased to move around the Forests eating the deer, and other ways were found of supporting it, although kings and their colleagues continued for centuries to be large eaters of salt venison.

In the mid thirteenth century, when records of individual Forests first become abundant, their original purpose was already in decline. Each Forest had its justices, wardens, Foresters-of-fee, verderers, regarders, foot-Foresters, riding-Foresters, etc. Some of these offices were hereditary; others were in the gift of the king or the local sheriff. They were supposed to supervise the Crown's interests in the Forests, and like other medieval administrators they did much of their business through the medium of special courts of law. In proportion to their dignity they enjoyed fees and perquisites of pasture-rights, timber, and wood, as well as opportunities for making profits in unofficial ways.

Conservation laws were formidable in theory: a Forest inhabitant was not supposed, *inter alia*, to cut down his own trees or grub out his private woodland or even to take dead wood. But the records of Forest officialdom portray an easy-going, incredibly slow, and apparently over-staffed system. Deterrent penalties were seldom imposed except for a small range of offences—for instance, in Essex the Foresters automatically confiscated any goats in the Forests. Most of the business of Forest courts was concerned with raising revenue from 'fines' which we would regard as income from taxes, fees, rents, and sales. A man 'stealing' trees might be 'fined', often years later, a sum roughly equal to their value. An offender who 'assarted'—appropriated for his own use—part of the Forest land was often allowed to keep his assart on payment of an annual rent. Even 'trespassers against the venison' were treated surprisingly leniently, seeing that deer were semi-agricultural animals and the king's private property. No less an offender than the Precentor of St Paul's, convicted on several poaching charges in 1277, got off with a short jail term and a fine of £2.75 Some regulations were particularly well adapted for collecting fees from people who did not wish to observe them; for instance, the requirement that dogs be 'expeditated' by cutting off part of one of the animal's feet lest it run after the deer.

As well as revenue—much of which was absorbed in the administration—Forests provided an inexpensive source of the perquisites and bounties which medieval kings dispensed out of piety, self-interest, or for reasons of state. These took the form of gifts of venison, of live deer for starting parks, of timber, of rights to assart, and of offices in the Forest hierarchy. Henry III's liberality with timber and deer led to an early, if temporary, conservation measure; in the Close Rolls for 1257 we find an order suspending such benefactions in a long list of Forests 'because of the destruction caused'.

Forest land-uses

During the Middle Ages the word 'Forest' came to mean, not the whole area within the Forest jurisdiction, but the 'waste of the Forest'—that is, the part of it which was not farmland, private woodland, or built up. When it is said that Waltham Forest once covered 60,000 acres, of which the present Epping Forest is only 6,000 acres, most of the difference is due to a change in the meaning of the word and not to actual encroachment.

Five land uses were widespread in Forest wastes: production of venison, grazing of farm animals, timber, wood from pollard trees, and underwood in coppices. The king normally owned the deer, but only some, if any, of the other rights. The grazing, and sometimes the wood, belonged wholly or partly to commoners. Private individuals might own the soil—with mineral rights—or the wood or timber.

Readers of Gilbert White's *Selborne* will recall the contrast in the eighteenth century between the twin Hampshire Forests, Alice Holt with its timber trees and the adjacent treeless Woolmer; this distinction seems to have been then at least 500 years old.[76] Epping is traditionally a Forest of pollards, in contrast to Enfield Chase which contained little but timber. The Forest of Wyre appears to have been mainly coppice. Coppices in Forests were usually intermittently grazed; for instance at Hatfield, Essex, the coppices were supposed to be grazed for the latter half of a rigid eighteen-year felling cycle.[77]

The Crown's interests in deer and in the Forest laws waned over the Middle Ages. The other land uses fought out their conflicts much as they did on any large common. Sixteenth-century Forest administration was poorly organized, and the Crown made little profit out of such wood and timber rights as remained to it.[78] Fortunately in 1565 Roger Taverner made a survey of many of the Forests and Crown woods, giving acreages, numbers of timber trees, and even details of underwood;[79] this was the first of a series of detailed surveys which are a most valuable historical source.

In the seventeenth century there was a revival of Crown interest. Charles I tried to resuscitate the Forest laws in the hope of making his subjects pay money to contract out of them. Some Forests were sold off to private individuals. But Forests where the Crown still owned the soil were seen as places where timber might be grown for naval purposes. Acts of Parliament were passed to allow other interests to be overridden, and between 1660 and 1700 some 11,000 acres of Dean and 1,400 acres of the New Forest were enclosed and planted. This was probably the first large-scale instance of modern forestry in Britain. Timber also became the overriding interest in Alice Holt and the Forest of Bere, Hampshire, but in other Forests, such as Sherwood, Nottinghamshire, and Woolmer, this phase had little effect. The new plantations were intended to make the Navy relatively independent of other supplies. Had they been adequately cared for, and had the Navy stopped growing, they might have achieved this objective. In the event, as Hart's figures show, the Forest of Dean supplied only about 3 per cent of the oak used by the Navy from 1762 to 1817; it is doubtful whether all the Forests together contributed as much as 10 per cent.

The Forests were the most complex instance in Britain of the multiple use of land, and the philosophy of the enclosure movement was particularly unsympathetic to them. The period 1770–1860 was the most destructive in their history.[11, 30] Much of what survived this phase still remains, although in many places the traditional land use has been replaced by coniferous plantations or spontaneous birch woodland.

The Forests as they are now

Only the New Forest survives in something like its medieval form as an institution. The Verderers still regularly hold the modern equivalent of the Court of Swainmote and Attachment, although by a historical inversion they are now appointed by, and uphold the rights of, the commoners and other interested parties, the rights of the Crown having devolved on the Forestry Commission. A shadow of the ancient administration lingers in Dean and Epping. Common rights are still exercised in these three Forests and elsewhere.

The coppice element in Forests was neglected early by the Crown, which never developed a proper organization for selling wood. The medieval coppices in the New Forest and Dean fell into decay by the seventeenth century, although numerous woodbanks remain in the former (Tubbs 1968). Pollarding, too, was discouraged in the belief that it conflicted with the timber interest. Many pollards survive in the New Forest, though not cut since the practice was prohibited in 1698, but with this exception coppices and pollards are now largely confined to Forests where the Crown did not own the wood rights.

Early maps make it clear that the physical boundaries of most Forests were not wood-shaped or park-shaped but had concave outlines, funnelling into roads, like other large commons. This can still be seen in the northern half of Epping Forest. Within the Forest, coppices might be defined by wood-banks, but otherwise there was no demarcation between areas of trees or scrub and treeless 'plains' or 'lawns' and heathland. Forests, like parks, contained lodges—sometimes in permanent embanked enclosures (Crawford 1954)—from which their business was carried on. A few of them were sufficiently grand for royal visits.

More is known about the vegetation history of Forests than of any other form of wood-pasture. The division into plains and areas of trees is of great antiquity: in the New Forest, for which there is some pollen evidence, it goes back to the Bronze Age, although—despite deterioration of the soil—the tree-land has fluctuated considerably. Regeneration of trees in unenclosed woods has been mainly by seed, and in consequence the present trees, where not planted, tend to reflect in their ages the history of grazing on the site. Tubbs shows that in the New Forest the unenclosed trees date either from 1663 to 1763, or from 1858 to 1923, or from after 1938, periods in which records show that grazing slackened. Heavy felling during the Commonwealth, and successful re-establishment of trees immediately after, are reported from a number of Forests.

Grazing is a highly selective influence, and is doubtless responsible for the relatively poor flora, with few tree species or plants specific to woodland, of Forests compared to nearby woods. The notable rarity of hazel, ash, and lime in unenclosed Forests is only partly explained by the poor soils of most such areas. Hazel is recorded in the New Forest coppices as late as the seventeenth century, and its disappearance is almost certainly due to grazing; like ash, it is a favourite food of cattle and deer. Holly is more resistant; it tends to increase in times of slack grazing and is now the commonest shrub in Forests on acid soils. Hawthorn is abundant in some Forests, although its young coppice shoots can be eaten. Holly used to be encouraged because its foliage was cut as iron rations for deer and other stock in winter. Both holly and thorn were valued as protection for young timber trees. Beech has also increased; in the New Forest it is much more abundant than it was 400 years ago, though it is not clear how far this is due to natural succession and how far to the selective felling of oak.

Old trees in Forests include such famous giants as the Major Oak in Sherwood. A few Forests contain large numbers of trees more than 300 years old, and are rich in creatures that live on ancient trees. The New Forest is exceptionally rich because its old trees grow over wide areas at variable spacings but often close together; there are plenty of dead trees and it is still relatively free from air pollution. Despite its chequered history, Rose and James regard it as the nearest modern approximation to the Wildwood in Western Europe in respect of those features that the more exacting tree-inhabiting lichens require.[80]

The Essex and Middlesex Forests

The six Forests of Essex, plus the royal chase of Enfield—a Forest in all but name—illustrate the variation in English Forests and their evolution. As an institution the Forest of Essex exercised a tenuous jurisdiction over most of the county until the thirteenth century; it was then reduced to Waltham Forest in the south-west, plus three smaller tracts based on the royal manors of Colchester, Writtle, and Hatfield Broadoak. Perambulations of the new legal boundaries make it clear that Essex was already a mainly agricultural county with hamlets, isolated farms, hedges, greens, minor roads, groves, and heathland. The Hatfield perambulation of 1298 would almost do for a description of the boundaries of that parish today.

These four *legal* Forests included six *physical* Forests (Fig. 26). All of these, together with Enfield Chase, were on poor agricultural land; except for Kingswood, they survived with numerous minor encroachments into the eighteenth century. They differed from each other in vegetation and management.

Kingswood, the first to disappear, was partly coppice and partly heath. Henry VIII granted it in 1535 to the burgesses of Colchester, who within a hundred years disposed of it to private individuals as farmland. Fragments of ancient woodland north of the town, which include lime and other characteristic plants, almost certainly still survive from the coppice.

Enfield Chase was part of an enormous tract of wood-pasture which stretched nine miles to Hatfield, Hertfordshire. The timber interest predominated to a greater extent, perhaps, than in any other Forest; at least from the sixteenth century there was practically no coppicing or pollarding.[81] As in some other Forests there was a heavy felling in the 1650s, followed by abundant regeneration of which we learn from a parliamentary inquiry in 1702.[82] In 1777 98 per cent of the Chase was enclosed, sold off, and grubbed out. The fragment that survives, Monken Hadley Common, is covered with maiden trees apart from a small area of

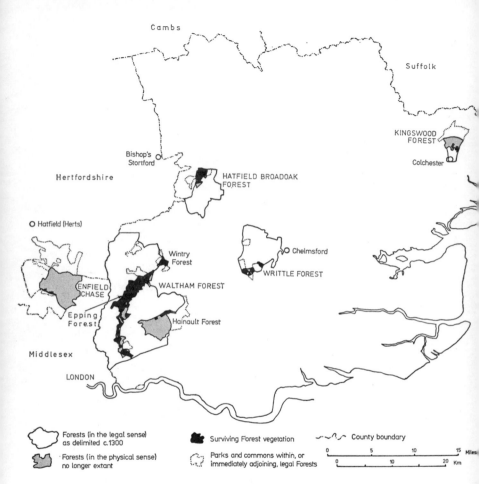

Fig. 26. Forests of Essex and Middlesex, showing the legal boundaries of Forest jurisdiction; the former extent of actual Forest vegetation; the extent of surviving uncultivated vegetation in Forests; the former extent of other kinds of wood-pasture.

plains; the almost total absence of pollards contrasts with Epping. It is dominated by beech on the higher gravels, through hornbeam, oak, and ash, with a little elm in a clayey bottom—a composition that closely reflects the 1702 description, though few of the trees are as old as that. There is practically no coppice.

Epping, Hainault (anciently Henholt), and Wintry (Fig. 24), latterly treated as an outlier of Epping, were mainly pollard and grazing Forests. They produced small amounts of timber, and in Epping a few giant beech stools indicate coppicing in the remote past; but pollarding, as the main tree management, was entrenched in manorial custom from at least the late Middle Ages.[83] These Forests are among the few frequently used for royal hunting. The commoners had rights to wood, as well as to the extensive grazing; but most of the pollard wood must have gone to the lords of the various manors and presumably found its way to London as firewood. Tree-ring and written evidence indicate an average pollarding cycle of about thirteen years.

In 1851 the Crown enclosed Hainault, where it owned most of the soil, wood, and timber as well as the deer; 92 per cent of the Forest disappeared with a speed that would have done credit to modern bulldozers. Epping and Wintry were saved from a similar fate by fragmented ownership and the tenacity of the commoners. Less than 10 per cent of their eighteenth-century area has disappeared. Such enclosures as were made were seldom grubbed out, and were revoked by the Epping Forest Act of 1878, which vested these Forests in the Corporation of London.

Epping Forest was one of the first areas to be deliberately managed as a 'wild' public open space. It is interesting to see what has happened to its historical features nearly a century later. The main tree species—beech, oak, hornbeam, holly—are much the same as they have been for at least 400 years. But the structure is very different, partly through deliberate policy and partly because the decline of traditional management has altered the competitive relations between plants.

Under the Act of 1878, the Corporation were required to 'preserve the natural aspect' of Epping Forest, an objective then evidently thought to be capable of definition and perhaps even of achievement. This phrase was interpreted to mean buying out and terminating the wood-cutting rights which, though declining, had been the means of frustrating the destruction of the Forest. Grazing rights were continued but have declined. It was the policy, especially in the early days, to promote maiden, rather than pollard, trees; to this end large numbers of pollards have been felled and natural seed regeneration encouraged in clearings.

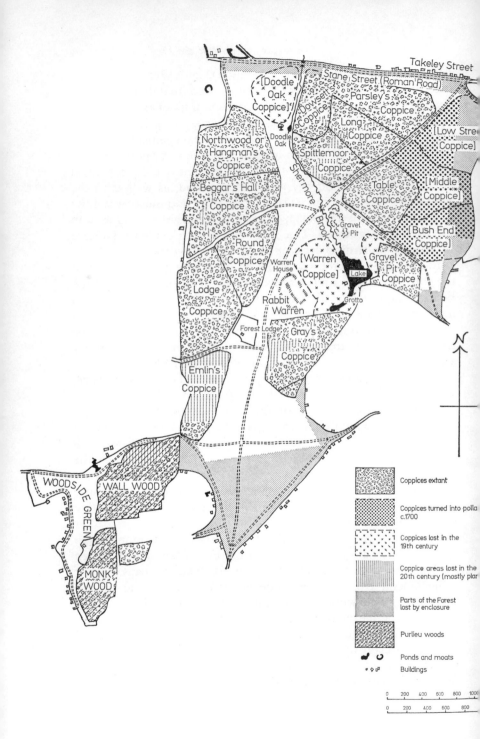

Takeley Street

Stane Street (Roman Road)

[Doodle Oak Coppice]

Dowsett's Coppice

Parsley's Coppice

Long Coppice

[Low Stre [Coppice]

Northwood or Hangman's Coppice

Doodle Oak

Spittlemoor Coppice

Shermore Brook

[Middle Coppice]

Beggar's Hall Coppice

Table Coppice

[Bush End Coppice]

Gravel Pit

Round Coppice

Warren House

[Warren Coppice]

Gravel Pit Coppice

Lake

Lodge Coppice

Rabbit Warren

Grotto

Forest Lodge

Gray's Coppice

Emlin's Coppice

N

WOODSIDE GREEN

WALL WOOD

MONK WOOD

	Coppices extant
	Coppices turned into polla c.1700
	Coppices lost in the 19th century
	Coppice areas lost in the 20th century (mostly plan
	Parts of the Forest lost by enclosure
	Purlieu woods
♪ ○	Ponds and moats
○ ♀ ⌂	Buildings

0   200   400   600   800   1000

0   200   400   600   800

These changes have had the effect of promoting timber trees at the expense of the more traditional features of the Forest. There are still many thousand pollards left, but they are overgrown; the beeches blow down easily, and they cast a shade beneath which nothing will grow. The supposed depredations of visitors provide a convenient, if doubtfully convincing, reason for the disappearance of plants like primroses and polypody, but hardly explain the decline of crab-apple and other small trees, or the death of oaks which fail to compete with unpollarded beech. The plains and scrub areas have greatly declined, invaded by birch and oak, and what is left or has been restored is chiefly grass rather than the heather which used to cover wide areas. We should not be too critical of the Conservators of the Forest: they would have done far worse had they taken the advice of the forestry or municipal-park interests rather than of men like E. N. Buxton, author of the classic *Epping Forest*, 1884. But the fact is that the historical features of the Forest have been diluted, and those that remain are now unstable. It is much to be hoped that the varied landscape of our ancestors will not be allowed to complete the process of turning into a large, but relatively dull, tract of secondary woodland.

Hainault Forest gives a rather better impression than Epping of what a pollard Forest used to look like. The trees in the surviving fragment are not so long out of the lopping rotation, and the plain and heathland elements survive or have been restored.

Hatfield is of supreme interest in that *all* the elements of a medieval Forest survive: deer, cattle, coppice woods, pollards, scrub, timber trees, grassland, and fen, plus a seventeenth-century lodge and rabbit warren. As such it is almost certainly unique in England and possibly in the world. The Crown's interest disappeared in the Middle Ages and it then had a chequered history in private hands. Although the usual conflicts of interest were sometimes resolved with sword and pistol, the

Fig. 27. Hatfield Forest, Essex. Small Forest with straggling concave outline, boundary houses, roads, coppices and former coppices. The plains between the coppices are grassland with areas of scrub and with scattered pollard trees. Also shown are Woodside Green—a smallish common with pollards—and the two medieval purlieu woods.

land-use history has been remarkably stable. In 1851 it came within an inch of sharing the fate of Hainault, but the greater part went as a single lot to the sympathetic Houblon family, who preserved it as a deer park. Only about 10 per cent—including, unfortunately, most of the original common-shaped boundary—was grubbed out.

The description at the head of the chapter, written by corrupt commissioners trying to destroy the Forest, still holds good 340 years later. The Forest consists of defined and embanked coppices round a central plain (Fig. 27). There were then 17 coppices, of which 12 survive at least in part. Three coppices were converted to tracts of pollards, chiefly hornbeam, in the early eighteenth century; 2 others, from which the underwood went in the nineteenth century and the timber in the twentieth, are now represented by faint earthworks and surviving elms. The plains contain pollards, some of them huge, chiefly oak, maple, and ash, and tracts of 'Bushie ground' with ancient hawthorns. In the early Middle Ages there were two 'purlieu woods'—exclaves to which some of the Forest laws applied—called Walwode and Monkenewode; both survive alongside the very beautiful Woodside Green with its pollards.

Apart from the lake—not a medieval reservoir but made about 1750—and a few fine specimen trees, the Forest owes very little to the last 250 years. For over a century its management has been in decline; the coppice fences have decayed, allowing deer and cattle access at all times, there has been some haphazard tree-planting in the plains, and of late years the bulldozer has made inroads on the coppices in well-meant attempts at 'renewal'. Nevertheless, it is in better condition than any other Forest; the grazing is kept up, and some of the coppices and even pollards were cut in the 1960s. Hatfield is the only place where one can step back into the Middle Ages to see, with only a small effort of the imagination, what a Forest looked like in use. It would be comparatively simple to restore it to full working order. Most of it belongs to the National Trust; let us hope that it will receive the sympathetic and scholarly treatment for which the Trust is famed in the restoration of historic properties.

And who has heard of Writtle Forest (Fig. 26)? Like Hatfield it has been in private hands for many centuries. It is not quite so well preserved—it appears to have lost the great pollard beeches that adorned it in the Middle Ages—but most of it is still there, and in the quiet of winter is a wild and lovely place. Nearly everything one sees there is of the fourteenth century or earlier: the great assart surrounded by hornbeam springs and alder slades; the heathland, pollard oaks, and wood-banks; the lonely cottage, with a palfrey grazing in its pightle, on the site of the hermitage where a solitary monk dwelt. This astonishing survival from the depths of the medieval countryside is within twenty-five miles of St Paul's Cathedral.

10   Trees on the farm: hedges and elsewhere

The grubbing up of Hedge Rows is become general, and the Growth
of Timber in them is thereby totally destroyed, owing to the great
Price given for Corn since the Bounty took place for exporting of
Corn and Beer, which gives every Farmer encouragement to grub
Hedge Rows up, and convert them into Corn Land.

House of Commons Journal, 1792, p. 318
[Grubbing of hedges was reported from 18 out of
38 counties; this entry is for Hampshire]

The antiquity of hedges

Few popular myths have been more pernicious than the notion
that all hedges date from the parliamentary enclosures. Although
the actual origin of hedges has never passed wholly into oblivion
the complex truth has rarely been fully appreciated, and it is only
within the last ten years that extensive work has been done on
what the hedges themselves have to tell us. Much of this work has
been summarized by Pollard, Hooper and Moore (1974) and will
not be repeated in detail here.

The maintenance of live hedges, as opposed to fences and
walls, appears in books and pamphlets on farming and in literary
works from the eleventh century onwards. The word gave rise to
such medieval derivatives as *hedgehog*, *hedge-sparrow*, and *hedging-bill*.
More specific references to hedges go back at least to the thirteenth
century; they usually record either the planting, or disputes about
the felling, of particular hedges. Live hedges, although familiar
in Anglo-Saxon times, increased steadily in numbers during the
Middle Ages. Tusser in 1557[84] distinguished between what was
already the Ancient Countryside, in which hedges were so
numerous as to be an important source of fuel, and the less-
hedged 'champion', later to be the Planned Countryside. But the

166

latter was by no means hedgeless, as records of the planting of a hedge at Gamlingay, Cambridgeshire, in 1330[85] and the destruction of one at Newton Longueville, Buckinghamshire, in 1288[65] illustrate.

Early large-scale maps show individual fields, and the better ones, such as that of Gamlingay in 1601,[54] distinguish hedges from other kinds of boundary. In Ancient Countryside a high proportion of the hedges shown in early maps (for example, Hintlesham, Suffolk, 1595[53]) coincide in detail with modern ones; even at Conington, Huntingdonshire, in the heart of enclosure-act country, Dr Max Hooper has shown that 62 per cent of the modern hedges were already there in 1595. Early landscape paintings and engravings, such as Hoefnagel's view of Norwich in 1580, nearly always depict hedges and hedgerow trees.

The map of Earl's Colne in 1598 (frontispiece) depicts the Ancient Countryside of Essex, with its small fields (average about 5 acres), its lanes and isolated farms, and the vast mileage of hedges, carefully distinguished from the few fences, palings and walls. The representation of trees is partly conventionalized— they cannot really have been so uniform in size and spacing—but the map is a witness to the existence of large numbers of hedgerow trees and of occasional hedges without trees, lines of trees remaining from former hedges, and trees standing in fields. The modern fields of Earl's Colne are much larger, but as late as 1950 about half the hedges shown in the frontispiece were still extant.

Most readers will know Dr Max Hooper's correlation between the age of a hedge and the number of shrub species in it. The shrub count—species defined according to a standard list—in a 30-yard length of hedge gives the approximate age in centuries. An enclosure-act hedge typically has one or two shrubs; an older hedge will be mixed; while a hedge with 10 or more shrubs in 30 yards is likely to be pre-Conquest. This is an empirical relation which holds good over a wide range of counties; it is surprising how little influence management or geology has on the composition of an old hedge. The reasons underlying Hooper's relation are complex and little understood. A complaint at Hatfield Broadoak, Essex, in 1443 about the felling of a hedge containing 'oak, ash, maples, white thorn & black' shows that mixed hedges already existed then. Exceptions to Hooper's rule arise from the tendency of some farmers to imitate existing hedges—to plant mixed hedges in areas where most of the hedges are already ancient and mixed—and from the tendency of some elms to invade hedges, just as they do woods, and to supplant the existing shrubs.

Mr David Dymond and Mr Colin Ranson have examined the dispersed parish of Rougham, W. Suffolk, which straddles the boundary between Ancient and Planned Countryside. In the middle stands the isolated church, surrounded by 2- and 3-species hedges resulting from enclosure of heath and open field by Act of 1813. Farther out is a belt of hedges with 7 to 9 species, representing early medieval enclosure; this still contains most of the hamlets and houses. On the outer fringes of the parish, and sometimes between settlements, the hedges are of 4 to 7 species, representing later assarts into wood-pasture or woodland. In the nearby parish of Felsham, Mrs Ann Hart has examined 298 hedges with an average of 7·3 (occasionally up to 14) species per 30-yard length. The highly dispersed settlement with 17 scattered moats makes it not unreasonable that the whole parish should have been hedged in the early Middle Ages; the fields, indeed, form an irregular grid pattern of the kind that is often conjectured to date from Roman times.

The great majority of hedges of all periods appear to have originated by planting. Some of the oldest hedges, with plenty of hazel, maple, and spindle, may have much in common with one of the local underwood types; but there are many kinds of woodland, for example, those with lime or oak underwood, that rarely have parallels in hedges. The ground vegetation even of ancient hedges usually differs widely from that of woods; for instance, cow-parsley, the most familiar of all hedgerow plants, is infrequent except in the most recent woods. A few hedges are the 'ghost' boundaries of woods that have disappeared; such 'woodland relict' hedges may contain the more strict woodland plants such as small-leaved lime, wood anemone, or (in the Midlands) dog's-mercury.

Hedgerow trees

Hedgerow trees are frequently referred to in medieval court rolls in the context of disputes about felling, obstruction of the highway, or public dangers such as 'one ancient & decayed [black] poplar growing out too far over the King's highway' at Great Canfield, Essex, in 1422.[86] Early maps—there are many Essex and Suffolk examples—often show individual hedgerow trees; and as far back as the Earl's Colne, Essex, map of 1598, part of which forms the frontispiece, we commonly find lines of trees across fields, evidently surviving from hedges that had already disappeared. Early landscape artists, such as Kip and his predecessors, often show hedgerow trees in great detail, with particular attention to variations of shape and spacing. The majority of hedges are remarkably close-set with trees, 10 yards or so

Table 4. Trees on 603 acres of farmland in Roxwell [87]

	Maiden	Pollard
Elm	370	1848
Oak	131	715
Ash	214	376
Maple	58	309
Willow	—	30
Hornbeam	10	—
	783	3278

apart, which we might attribute to artistic licence were they not confirmed by numerical surveys. A typical example is that of three farms in Roxwell, Essex, which in 1734 had 6·7 trees per acre of farmland (Table 4). Large as these numbers may seem, this is by no means an extreme case: at Thorndon, E. Suffolk, *c.* 1742 a farm of 187 acres had no less than 6,058 pollard trees.[88] At a reasonable estimate from these and other surveys, in Essex and Suffolk in the early eighteenth century there were between 4 and 8 hedgerow trees to every acre of farmland, at least five times as many as there are now.

Hedgerow trees might be either timber or pollards. The terms of farm leases usually reserved the timber for the landlord—apart from the tenant's housebote—but gave the pollard wood to the tenant. Pollards are usually described from the landlord's point of view and therefore in disapproving terms. The Thorndon farm was, not unnaturally, 'very much incumbered' with pollards 'and if a great deal more was cut down it would be much better for the Land'. Hedges sometimes provided large or curved timber for buildings. As early as 1608–9, when over half of the 'hooks', 'knees', etc. taken from Crown estates in eastern England are recorded as coming from trees in fields,[89] hedges were a principal source of special shipbuilding timbers.

From about 1750 there appears to have been a steady decline in hedgerow timber in the Ancient Countryside, which—rightly or wrongly—alarmed the Navy by 1792. Timber trees were planted in many of the enclosure-act hedges, but we do not know whether this was an adequate compensation.

We know little of the parts which deliberate policy and natural accident have played in the origin of the present hedgerow trees. Trees are usually of the same age as the hedge or younger; very rarely does a hedge incorporate trees older than itself. It is not known how many trees in enclosure-act hedges are the ones originally planted there. There are many records of trees having been planted in existing hedges, but we do not know how many were established in this way and how many arose from the saplings, elm suckers, or coppice shoots with which a mixed hedge abounds.

Hedgerow pollards and timber trees show a good deal of regional variation. Oak, for instance, predominates in most of Norfolk, elm in Essex, and ash in the N.E. Midlands. This is not well correlated with either the timber trees or underwood in local woods. The hornbeam woods of Essex have their parallels in Forest pollards, but hornbeam is not common in field hedges. Oak is less often predominant as a timber tree in hedges than in woods, despite being easier to grow. Hedgerow trees evidently express a different set of historical and ecological factors from those which operate in woods.

Hedgerow pollards still exist in tens of thousands in eastern England, but are uncommon elsewhere. They very seldom occur in enclosure-act hedges, since the practice of pollarding was in decline by the time of the enclosures; but it is not clear why there should be so few pollards in the ancient hedges of the Welsh Border or Devon.

Trees of settlements

The most interesting of the ancient trees of settlements are the elms. Gnarled elm pollards are a characteristic feature of many villages and hamlets—or of places where such have been—in East Anglia and the East Midlands. At Knapwell, Cambridgeshire, we find vast pollard elms, of surrealist shapes, marking the deserted streets and closes of the shrunken medieval village (Plate XIII). One occasionally finds distinctive settlement elms in other districts, as on the Lizard Peninsula, Cornwall, where nearly every one of more than a hundred settlements and deserted settlements has its grove of one of the three local elm varieties.

Richens (1967, etc.) has analysed the different sorts of elms in village closes in a number of counties. He concludes that there has been a series of fashions in elms, for planting round houses, going back to the Iron Age. Elms, introduced to habitation sites in this way, are nearly impossible to get rid of and have maintained their distinctive characters ever since.

While no study of a deserted settlement is complete without a glance at its elms, other trees may be of interest too. Such, for instance, are the oak and ash pollards on the earthworks of Lindsey Castle, Suffolk, which may go back to the time when it was inhabited.

Trees in fields and meadows

The practice of growing pollard willows on the banks of rivers is first recorded in the thirteenth century[90] and was important especially in the Fens, which had little other wood. Nowadays this is the most active branch of pollarding; individual trees seem seldom to be of any great age and new pollards are still occasionally formed. With this exception, few now remain of the innumerable trees that before 1750 used to stand on their own in fields and meadows. Many of these were pollards, and occasionally they were very large, as some of their survivors are. In West Donyland, Essex, in 1393, John Gru was prosecuted for 'cutting the branches of an ancient oak', a gigantic tree since the branches made 1,200 billets, which would have been about

2½ tons of firewood.[91] The black poplar still grows mainly in meadows and pastures rather than in hedges, and the ploughing up of these sites probably explains its present rarity.

Wood-pasture versus farmland

Nowadays we have far more trees in Forests and parks than in the country at large, but this has not always been so. In 1783, for instance, the *wooded* parts of the New Forest averaged 6·3 timber trees per acre (Tubbs 1968), a density often exceeded on ordinary farmland. It is somewhat surprising, therefore, to find so clear a distinction between wood-pasture and farmland in respect of tree lichens.

There is one place where one can still see the trees of an ordinary seventeenth-century countryside. At Ickworth, W. Suffolk, the great park—now National Trust—is set with some of the most imposing pollard oaks and other ancient trees in England; the casual visitor might suppose it to be a medieval deer park thinly disguised with boundary groves and Capability-Brownery around the house. Not so: Ickworth parish, which roughly coincides with the park, was described field by field in 1665, and then consisted of various hamlets and greens, numerous hedged fields, groves, and a small open field.[92] In 1701 the whole parish was depopulated and emparked, and all its trees, some of them already ancient, thereby preserved. There are trees on hedge-banks, elms in the boundaries of closes, trees in former gardens, and trees that must once have stood in fields. A ring-count in a fallen elm confirms that it was last pollarded, as one might expect, around 1690.

11 Destruction and conservation: the ancient woods since 1945

Parkhurst Forest . . . is a very good example of what a national forest ought *not* to be, and of what the New Forest would have become had the old Act empowering its inclosure as a State timber farm not been modified. It is an ancient royal forest; but instead of remaining in its natural condition of a wild furze heath and woodland it is now a solid mass of timber, mainly oak and chestnut, viewless, and almost impenetrable except by the roads cut through it. If any one desires to know how dull a thousand acres of scientific plantation can be he need only spend an hour in Parkhurst Forest. On the other hand it is an economic success.

C. J. Cornish, *The New Forest and the Isle of Wight*, 1898

Recent destruction of woodland and trees

The thirty years since 1945 have been a time of unprecedented destruction of ancient woodland, in contrast to the active conservation or slow decline of the previous thousand years. This sort of thing has often been said before, but this time it is real. Earlier damage was usually reversible. This time it is not a matter of felling trees which will grow again, but of converting sites to other uses. It is an uncanny experience to trace an identifiable wood or hedge through five or seven centuries, and on going to the spot to be just in time for the dying embers of the bonfires in which it has been destroyed.

Evidence of destruction is all around us, but to measure it would require a considerable research programme. Successive Forestry Commission censuses [93] were not compiled for this purpose and are of little use to us. To a forester, a 'wood' includes anything from an orchard-like poplar plantation, designed for a life of some forty years, upwards; and ancient woodland forms an unknown fraction of various categories from Broadleaved High

173

Forest to Unutilizable Scrub. At best we get such unhelpful generalizations as the reported increase in the total area of what is deemed to be 'broadleaved woodland' in some regions—as if the planting of a thousand acres of poplars in Lakenheath Fen, Suffolk, somehow compensated for the destruction of Lineage, Spelthorne, Hinderclay, and Pakenham Woods, Stanstead Great Wood, and Assington Thicks.

Peterken and Harding (1975), going through Rockingham Forest, Northamptonshire, wood by wood, show that 42 per cent by area of the ancient woodland which remained in 1946 has since lost its characteristics, almost entirely through being replanted with conifers or grubbed out altogether. Their similar studies in central Lincolnshire and W. Cambridgeshire show losses of 46 per cent and 36 per cent. From an analysis by C. E. Ranson in mid Suffolk I estimate that nearly half the ancient woodland went in the same period. These losses in a mere thirty years are certainly unprecedented. In some cases, as with the great woods of Bury St Edmunds Abbey, the destruction in the 1950s and 1960s equalled that in the whole of the previous 400 years. Even in absolute terms, it is unlikely that there has been a thirty-year period since the Conquest in which, as in all these districts except W. Cambridgeshire, 1½ per cent of the whole land area has ceased to be native woodland. Fig. 15 illustrates what this means for a specific piece of country.

Casual observation suggests that a similar story could be told of nearly every sheet of the Ordnance Survey: of Dorset, the steep oak woods of mid Wales, the Wye gorge, the Forest of Wyre, the hilltop woods of the Welsh Border, and the romantic lichen-hung corkscrew oaks of the deep valleys of Dartmoor and Bodmin Moor. The long arm of destruction has reached from the Lizard Peninsula to remote Argyll. An estimate of a third of the ancient woodland destroyed in thirty years is not unreasonable. In the larger woods and some better-wooded areas it may exceed 50 per cent. The bulk of the loss has been to afforestation, followed by agriculture. Quarrying comes well behind, while the inroads of housing, roads, and industry are generally insignificant in acreage. 'Public pressure' is rarely a major threat: most ancient woods are very resistant to damage by visitors, except perhaps where they abut directly on built-up areas, for instance, Birchanger Wood, Bishop's Stortford, Hertfordshire.

I have treated forestry as one among many changes of land use which have destroyed the historical value of woodland. This need not have been so: most new plantations are on former moorland or heath or the sites of earlier plantations, and some of the Forestry Commission's most successful enterprises, such as Thetford Forest, Norfolk, have not touched a single acre of ancient woodland. Afforestation seldom sweeps away all evidence that an ancient wood ever existed, as do ploughing or quarrying; but the processes of getting rid of the trees that are already there, and of preventing their regrowth from competing with the planted trees, more or less severely damage the underwood and ground vegetation on which the biological continuity depends. The existing trees may be dug out with bulldozers, felled, ring-barked, or poisoned (usually in combination). Stanstead Great Wood (Fig. 15) was defoliated by spraying 2,4,5-T from a helicopter,[94] although latterly it is no longer thought good to let this chemical loose on the countryside. Not all the existing trees may be destroyed at once, but those that remain cease to be a crop and become a nuisance. The forester's job is to grow timber, not wood.

When a wood is 'coniferized', the ground vegetation may flourish for a few years, but after the conifers have closed in, their dense evergreen shade and heavy leaf-litter make it almost impossible for anything to grow under them and reduce the original vegetation to remnants along rides. Replanting with pure oak, beech, or sycamore is not quite so destructive, but their shade and rot-resistant dead leaves are also harmful to underwood and ground vegetation. Much of the interest of traditional woods containing oak or beech depends on what grows *between* these trees rather than *under* them, and many of our duller woods are those converted to pure oak or beech a century or more ago (pages 126–7).

The effects of intensive replanting of ancient woods range from almost total destruction—apart, perhaps, from the earthworks, the site might just as well be growing barley—to moderate damage. The existing trees may refuse to die (small-leaved lime resists ring-barking and poisoning) and honey-fungus or rabbits may carve out gaps in the new ones. The coniferized part of Chalkney Wood, Essex, is, for the moment, by no means a write-off; the plantation is patchy and much of the underwood survives. But on the whole destruction predominates in woods planted with conifers, while those planted with broad-leaved trees are usually damaged only.

The underwood trades have continued to decline. They now survive mainly in the south, and the most flourishing, the chestnut paling industry, is perhaps the least interesting in terms of woodmanship. Unused woods tend to fall into silvicultural neglect, but this is the least serious vicissitude that can befall them. A neglected wood loses some of its historical interest, but the decline is slow, and as Cambridgeshire experience has shown it is reversible. A multitude of groves is maintained for shooting or fox-hunting, without which they would vanish almost overnight (a point which opponents of these activities would do well to remember).

The destruction of hedges will be familiar to most readers. Estimates of the rate of destruction vary widely owing to differences between regions and to the difficulty of deciding when a damaged hedge becomes a destroyed one. The problem is at its worst in the cornlands of eastern England, where parish after parish—particularly in the richly hedged Ancient Landscape of Suffolk and north Essex—now has well under half the hedges shown on the 2½-inch map. Much of the west and north still has a relatively complete hedge system. The loss of hedgerow trees is even faster than that of hedges, though it has perhaps been exaggerated in the belief that stag-head of oak (page 25) is necessarily a fatal condition. The ravages of the current Dutch Elm Disease epidemic have been most severe in *Ulmus procera* (English Elm) in hedges; it has made much less headway among the archaeologically more interesting elms or in woods.

The destruction of Forests and commons is probably less severe than it was 150 years ago; but that of parks has been rapid and is closely connected with the decline of country houses. Even if the great trees are left standing when a park is ploughed, the plough plays havoc with their roots, while fertilizers and sprays poison the plants and animals living on them.

Attitudes to conservation

The problems outlined above are not confined to Britain. A century ago, coppicing and pollarding were widespread from Sweden to the Mediterranean and from Portugal to Tibet; now they are everywhere in decline and survive mainly in southern Europe.

After the destruction of Hainault Forest by the tail-end of the enclosure movement, the idea began to grow in public opinion that the amenities of the countryside could no longer safely be left in the hands of commercial interests alone. The quotation at the head of the chapter expresses this view. The Victorians evidently imagined that 'wild heath and woodland' were in some sense the 'natural condition' of Royal Forests; we have already seen the consequences of applying this opinion to Epping Forest. More recently, this public amenity interest in the conservation of trees and woodlands has been joined by the interest of biologists and naturalists, expressed by public bodies such as the Nature Conservancy Council and voluntary bodies such as the county naturalists' trusts. In recent years, with the rise of interest in rural history as a practical, and not a purely literary, field of study, the archaeological importance of woods and trees is becoming more widely known. Even a derelict Bury St Edmunds Abbey wood is as much an ancient monument as are the Abbey ruins which the Department of the Environment lovingly maintains; and in the Bradfield Woods we actually get a chance to see an aspect of the Middle Ages—as essential then as coal and oil are now—in working order.

These three conservation interests by no means coincide. A grove of beeches planted by a Regency squire on the top of a chalk down may be held sacred by the amenity faction. The naturalists, knowing that it harbours little but pigeons and nettles, may not share this enthusiasm. The archaeologist may want to get rid of it before its roots have completed the destruction of the Iron Age hill-fort on which it stands. On the whole, however, these interests are usually in sympathy at the local level. Over matters such as the preservation of a particular bluebell wood they are often allied. In matters of national policy, however, the more influential spokesmen of the amenity interest often show little understanding of historical processes or detailed sympathy with the wildlife interest. The idea that the countryside is somehow 'natural' has given way to the equally dubious notion that it is wholly artificial. The planting of new groves is thought to be an adequate remedy for failure to conserve existing woods and trees. The slogans 'The Countryside is Continually Changing' and 'Conservation Doesn't Mean Preservation' are too often used without investigating how far they are true in particular cases. The claims of woodland conservation are supposed to be met by a general exhortation to plant oak instead of pine.

The 'Plant a Tree in '73' campaign illustrates what can go wrong. The objective—to remedy a general lack of young non-woodland trees—was wholly laudable, and in many circumstances planting would be the best or only way to achieve it. But the campaign was unduly hurried. There were difficulties about where the trees to be planted were to come from or who was to water them afterwards. More often than not, they were a meaningless assortment of whatever came to hand, with the usual over-emphasis on flowering cherries and hybrid limes. The black poplar, that most grandly rugged of all native trees, not to be matched exactly anywhere outside Britain, continued to decline towards extinction for lack of interest. There was little investigation of why there were not already enough young trees. Any mixed hedge is full of sapling trees, which are destroyed by hedge-cutting or burning before they can reach pole size; adding a few extra saplings is no answer. It may be argued that such exercises as planting elms in a hedge already chock-a-block with perfectly good elm suckers merely waste money and do no real harm; but although the campaign did achieve something it absorbed much public good-will on failures and side-issues.

These criticisms do not apply to everyone concerned with the public amenity interest. A notable exception is Essex County Council, which has an impressive record of determination and success in maintaining the woodland and trees of a hard-pressed county, and whose booklet (1974) on historic features in the countryside is a model of its kind.

The strategy of conservation

According to the Oxford English Dictionary, *conservation* means 'preservation from destructive influences, natural decay, or waste'. The impact and importance of these three factors will vary widely from site to site, and prescriptions, or even principles, hatched in some far-away office are unlikely to be right. Here I can do no more than mention some of the questions which should run in the mind of the would-be conservationist.

In most cases the immediate threat is one of 'waste', of deliberate destruction, sometimes for good reasons, sometimes for bad. We may reluctantly sympathize with those who convert woods to good plantations or good farmland, though there are now few opportunities left for doing this. It is harder to forgive the greedy optimism that deprived Londoners of Enfield Chase and Hainault Forest in exchange for a few square miles of poor farmland. We can have more sympathy with the farmer who amalgamates three two-acre fields than with his neighbour who every year cuts down a hedge between two 100-acre fields out of mere tidy-mindedness or to give his men something to do after the autumn sowing.

On a national scale, the best deterrent to waste is a revival of use. Even as I write, underwood has been re-invented by Inter-Technology Corporation—they call it British Thermal Unit Bushes—as an answer to the American energy crisis; 95 and in this country the neglect of the fuel and paper-pulp potential of underwood shows signs of coming to an end. Woods on the whole may be rather less productive of cellulose than plantations, but they cost nothing in planting, weeding, and thinning.

At a more specific level, it is obvious from the gaps in this book that much surveying needs to be done. Woods are historical documents that should be read before somebody burns them. We also need to identify the important sites on which to concentrate further action. For lack of such a survey we came within an inch of losing the Bradfield Woods; and the Writtle example (page 164) shows how substantial remains even of Royal Forests can lurk undetected in these crowded islands. Peterken (1974a) has introduced the idea of 'non-recreatability' as a guide for naturalists in selecting sites for conservation. Ancient coppice woods, wood-pastures, old secondary woodland and to some extent the older hedges all have features which once destroyed cannot in practice be re-created; biological as well as archaeological interests are served by concentrating on such places rather than on others whose destruction is readily reversible.

Practically any wood on an ancient site has some non-recreatable features. Its value will be enhanced if it is a complete medieval wood; if it contains several different types of native woodland; if its underwood is well preserved; if different parts of it have different origins or management histories; if it has earthworks that tell some particular story; if it has had some recent management, at least along rides; and if it has uncommon trees or other plants or interesting elms. The naturalist will usually prefer woods on ill-drained sites for their richer flora and fauna, and will value old timber trees and dead wood, although these last are not usually traditional features of woodland. The supremely valuable sites, such as the Bradfield Woods and Hatfield Forest, combine several of these factors and also have detailed historical documents which give meaning to their present features. The value of an ancient wood may be reduced by recent or past replanting, by having too many timber trees, or by long neglect. Large fragments, such as Hinderclay Wood (Fig. 19h) which has lost all its medieval boundary, may be less valuable than small but complete woods.

There is a pressing need for the preservation of series of woods chosen to illustrate the variation of woodland types and management in a district. To some extent this has been achieved in North Wales by the Nature Conservancy Council and in W. Cambridgeshire by the county Naturalists' Trust, but it is badly wanted in other areas of variable woodland.

Granted the desirability of forestalling the destruction of selected woods and other tree-land, what do we do with them? What does 'conservation' mean in the context of living things? The Bradfield Woods have been managed uninterruptedly for at least 700 years, and there is no obvious reason why they should not last a further 700; total preservation in their present state is a perfectly reasonable conservation objective. More often a medieval wood will have been neglected for between twenty and a hundred years. Some of its historic features will have been eroded through natural changes, but provided the coppice structure remains it should be capable of recovery if management is resumed. If this is not practicable, the next best solution may be to do nothing. Any third course of action may well erode the historic features faster than further neglect. An acceptable compromise will often be, as at Hayley Wood, to resume coppicing on part of the wood and to leave the remainder for the present.

It is more difficult to know what to do with ancient wood-pasture trees. Little is known about how to prolong their lives; since their virtue lies in their age and in the effects of past pollarding the problem is not solved merely be establishing young trees as successors. Effective conservation measures must include renewed pollarding of existing trees, if not too long neglected, and starting new pollards to be the very old trees of future centuries. To sacrifice ancient trees for the sake of a 'balanced' distribution of ages, as was proposed in 1971 for the New Forest, is to get the priorities wrong; there will always be middle-aged trees, but old trees, and big dead ones, are rare and precious.

Natural decay is seldom an imminent threat calling for precipitate action. To do nothing is seldom the best conservation policy, but will often be second best; it is easy to spend money on achieving a worse result. Planting trees, even of deciduous species, on a site not positively known to have been so treated before is a dilution of the historical evidence. Unless very carefully planned it destroys the existing vegetation patterns, and replaces the traditional variation of wild trees, on which much of the character of ancient woods depends, with the genetic monotony of commercial stock.

Abbreviations

B.C.	*Biological Conservation*
E.H.R.	*Economic History Review*
F.	*Forestry*
J.E.	*Journal of Ecology*
M.C.O.R.	Merton College, Oxford, Records
N.C.	*Nature in Cambridgeshire*
N.P.	*New Phytologist*
P.R.O.	Public Record Office
Q.J.F.	*Quarterly Journal of Forestry*
R.O.	Record Office
V.A.	*Vernacular Architecture*

Bibliography

There is no general book on the archaeology of woodland and trees. I give here a selection of works, touching on parts of the subject or dealing with particular regions and places, which the reader may find of interest. These are referred to in the text by author's name and date.

Ailesbury, Marquess of (1962). *A history of Savernake Forest*. Devizes.

Anderson, M. L. (1967). *A history of Scottish forestry*. London. Nelson.

Beevor, H. E. (1924). 'Norfolk woodlands, from the evidence of contemporary chronicles'. *Transactions of the Norfolk and Norwich Naturalists' Society*, **11**, 488–508.

Birks, H. J. B., Deacon, J., and Peglar, S. (1975). 'Pollen maps for the British Isles 5,000 years ago'. *Proceedings of the Royal Society, London B*, **189**, 87–105.

' *British Oak*' here and in the references means M. G. Morris and F. H. Perring (eds.), *The British Oak*, Classey (1974).

Coles, J. M., Hibbert, F. A., and Orme, B. J. (1973). 'Prehistoric roads and tracks in Somerset: 3. The Sweet track'. *Proceedings of the Prehistoric Society*, **39**, 256–93.

Crawford, O. G. S. (1954). *Archaeology in the field*. revised ed. Phoenix House.

Darby, H. C. (1971). *The Domesday geography of Eastern England*. Cambridge. (Parallel volumes for other regions.)

Edlin, H. L. (1973). *Woodland crafts in Britain*. 2nd ed. David & Charles.

Essex landscape: historic features (1974). Essex County Council.

Godwin, H. E. (1968). 'Organic deposits of Old Buckenham Mere, Norfolk.' *N.P.*, **67,** 95–107.

Godwin, H. E. (1975). *History of the British flora.* 2nd ed. Cambridge.

Hadfield, M. (1967). *Landscape with trees.* Country Life.

Harding, P. T. *See under* Peterken (1975).

Hart, C. E. (1966). *Royal forest: a history of Dean's woods as producers of timber.* Clarendon.

Hooper, M. D. *See under* Pollard.

McCracken, E. (1971). *The Irish woods since Tudor times.* David & Charles.

Merton, L. F. (1970). 'The history and status of woods on the Derbyshire limestone.' *J.E.*, **58,** 723–44.

Mitchell, A. F. (1974). *A field guide to the trees of Britain and northern Europe.* Collins.

Moore, N. W. *See under* Pollard.

Pennington, W. (1969). *The history of British vegetation.* English Universities Press.

Peterken, G. F. (1969). 'Development of vegetation in Staverton Park, Suffolk.' *Field Studies*, **3,** 1–39.

Peterken, G. F. (1974a). 'Developmental factors in the management of British woodlands'. *Q.J.F.*, **68,** 141–9.

Peterken, G. F. (1974b). 'A method for assessing woodland flora for conservation using indicator species'. *B.C.*, **6,** 239–45.

Peterken, G. F., and Harding, P. T. (1975). 'Woodland conservation in Eastern England: comparing the effects of changes in three study areas since 1946'. *B.C.* (in press).

Pettitt, P. A. J. (1968). *The royal forests of Northamptonshire, 1558–1714.* Northamptonshire Record Society.

Pollard, E., Hooper, M. D., and Moore, N. W. (1974). *Hedges.* Collins.

Prince, H. C. (1958). 'Parkland in the English landscape'. *Amateur Historian*, **3,** 332–49.

Rackham, O. (1969). 'Knapwell Wood.' *Nature in Cambridgeshire*, **12,** 25–31.

Rackham, O. (1971). 'Historical studies and woodland conservation'. *The scientific management of animal and plant communities for conservation*, ed. E. Duffey and A. S. Watt, 563–80. Nature Conservancy.

Rackham, O. (1972). 'Grundle House: on the quantities of timber in certain East Anglian buildings in relation to local supplies'. *V.A.*, **3**, 3–8.

Rackham, O. (1974). 'The oak tree in historic times'. *British Oak*, pp. 62–79.

Rackham, O. (1975). *Hayley Wood, its history and ecology*. Cambridgeshire and Isle of Ely Naturalists' Trust.

Richens, R. H. (1967). 'Essex elms'. *F.*, **40**, 185–206. (Includes a list of earlier papers on other counties.)

Roden, D. (1968). 'Woodland and its management in the medieval Chilterns'. *F.*, **41**, 59–71.

Rose, F. (1974). 'The epiphytes of oak'. *British Oak*, pp. 250–73.

Smith, A. H. (1956). *English place-name elements*. Cambridge.

Steele, R. C., and Welch, R. C. (1973). *Monks' Wood*. Nature Conservancy Council.

Steven, H. M., and Carlisle, A. (1959). *The native pinewoods of Scotland*. Edinburgh.

Tansley, A. H. (1939). *The British Islands and their vegetation*. Cambridge.

Tittensor, R. M. (1970). 'History of the Loch Lomond oakwoods'. *Scottish Forestry*, **24**, 100–18.

Troup, R. S. (1952). *Silvicultural systems*. 2nd ed. Oxford.

Tubbs, C. R. (1968). *The New Forest: an ecological history*. David & Charles.

Watt, A. S. (1924). 'The development and structure of beech communities on the Sussex Downs'. *J.E.*, **12**, 145–204.

Welch, R. C. *See under* Steele.

References

A list of the principal manuscripts and more specialized publications used in this book.

1 Gonner, E. C. K. *Common land and inclosure*. Macmillan (1912).
2 Mitchell, A. F. 'Dating the "ancient" oaks'. *Q.J.F.*, 60 (1966), 271–6.
3 An example of the many medieval records of the three poplars is in Suffolk (Bury St Edmunds) R.O. E2/9/1, dated 1310, which mentions *popeler* and *abel*.
4 Birks, H. H. A radiocarbon-dated pollen diagram from Loch Maree, Ross and Cromarty. *N.P.*, 71 (1972) 731–54.
5 Smith, A. G. 'The influence of Mesolithic and Neolithic man on British vegetation'. *Studies in the vegetational history of the British Isles*, ed. D. Walker and R. G. West, Cambridge (1970), pp. 81–96.
6 Turner, J. 'The *Tilia* decline: an anthropogenic interpretation.' *N.P.*, 61 (1962), 328–41.
7 Coles, J. *Archaeology by experiment*. Hutchinson (1973).
8 Turner, J. 'The anthropogenic factor in vegetation history. I. Tregaron and Whixall Mosses'. *N.P.*, 63, 73–90.
9 Liversidge, J. *Britain in the Roman empire*. Routledge (1968).
10 Taylor, C. C. *The Dorset landscape*. Hodder (1970).
11 Emery, F. *The Oxfordshire landscape*. Hodder (1974).
12 Turner, J. 'Post-Neolithic disturbance of British vegetation.' *Studies in the vegetational history* . . . (reference 5), 97–116.
13 The texts of most charters are published in J. M. Kemble, *Codex diplomaticus*, London (1839), and W. de G. Birch, *Cartularium Saxonicum*, London (1885–93). Commentaries

References

are provided by C. R. Hart, *The early charters of Eastern England*, Leicester (1966), and companion volumes for other regions.

14 Grundy, G. B. *Saxon charters of Worcestershire.* Birmingham Archaeological Society (1931).

15 Lennard, R. 'The destruction of woodland in the eastern counties under William the Conqueror'. *E.H.R.*, **15** (1945), 36–43.

16 Archibald, J. F. 'Wistman's Wood—a problem oakwood'. *British Oak*, p. 357.

17 *Cal. Close Rolls* and *Cal. Liberate Rolls* passim. I am indebted to the Department of the Environment and to Dr J. M. Fletcher for an opportunity to examine these timbers.

18 P.R.O. E143/9/2.

19 Three copies exist: British Museum Cott. Claud. C. xi; Gonville and Caius College Cambridge MS 485–9; and (an inferior MS) Ely Diocesan Registry (in Cambridge University Library) G/3/27.

20 Rackham, O. 'Medieval woodland areas'. *N.C.*, **11** (1968), 22–5.

21 Pembroke College, Cambridge, I, 1–3.

22 Salzman, L. F. *Building in England down to 1540.* 2nd ed. Clarendon (1967).

23 Venables, C. J. 'Uses of oak, past and present'. *British Oak*, pp. 113–22.

24 Harris, R. 'Poplar crucks in Worcestershire and Herefordshire'. *V.A.*, **5** (1974), 25.

25 M.C.O.R., 5342–5499.

26 Essex R.O., D/Db L1/9/4.

27 I am indebted for this analysis to Dr H. J. B. Birks, Mr P. Adam, and Mrs H. Prentice.

28 E.g. *Cal. Inq. Misc.*, **5**, no. 56 (1388).

29 *Cal. Liberate Rolls.*

30 Steane, J. M. *The Northamptonshire landscape.* Hodder (1974).

31 Essex R.O. D/DQ 16/1.

32 Lord Tollemache's muniments at Helmingham Hall; Ashburnham, Petre, and other collections in Essex and Suffolk (Ipswich) R.Os.

33 Brown, E. H., and Hopkins, S. V. 'Seven centuries of the

188

prices of consumables, compared with builders' wage-rates'. *Economica* **23** (1956), 296*ff.*

34 Rogers, J. T. *History of Agriculture and prices*, **3** & **4** (1872), **5** & **6** (1887).

35 P.R.O. SP/14/42 (with some corrections for confusion between returns per year and per coppice cycle).

36 Flinn, M. W. 'Timber and the advance of technology: a reconsideration'. *Annals of Science*, **15** (1959), 109–20.

37 Hammersley, G. 'The charcoal iron industry and its fuel', 1540–1740. *E.H.R. 2nd ser.*, **26** (1973), 593–613.

38 Schubert, H. R. *History of the British iron and steel industry*. London (1957).

39 Brandon, P. *The Sussex landscape*. Hodder (1974).

40 Yarranton, A. *England's improvement by sea and land*. (1677).

41 Birks, H. H. 'A pollen diagram from Abernethy Forest, Inverness shire'. *J F.*, **58** (1970), 827–46.

42 Edlin, H. L. *Trees, woods and man*. 3rd ed. Collins (1970).

43 Rubner, K. *Die pflanzengeographische Grundlage des Waldbaues*. Radebeul (1960).

44 Ketton-Cremer, R. W. *Felbrigg*. Hart-Davis (1962).

45 Pitt-Rivers, A. H. *King John's House*. (1890.)

46 Information derived chiefly from *House of Commons Journals*, *Navy Lists*, and article 'Shipping' by T. V. O'Connor in *Encyclopaedia Britannica*, 14th ed. (1929).

47 Merriman, R. D. *Queen Anne's navy*. Navy Records Society (1961).

48 James, W., and Malcolm, J. *General view of the agriculture of the county of Buckingham*. London (1794).

49 Wilson, M. 'The oak mildew'. *Transactions of the Royal Scottish Arboricultural Society*, **36** (1922), 92–7.

50 Essex R.O. D/DB T15/8.

51 Essex R.O. D/DSm.

52 Cambridgeshire R.O.

53 Ryan, G. H., and Redstone, L. J. *Timperley of Hintlesham*. Methuen (1931).

54 M.C.O.R. 6/17.

55 Essex R.O.

56 *Liber memorandorum ecclesiae de Bernewelle*, ed. J. W. Clarke. Cambridge (1907).

References

57 Tollemache B1/11 (*see* note 32).
58 Royal Commission on Historical Monuments, *West Cambridgeshire* (1968), lxvi-lxix.
59 Prince, H. C. 'The origin of pits and depressions in Norfolk'. *Geography*, **49** (1964), 15–32.
60 Dimbleby, G. W. *The development of British heathlands and their soils.* Oxford (1962).
61 Hawksworth, D. L. (ed.). *The changing flora and fauna of Britain.* Academic Press (1974).
62 Woodruffe-Peacock, E. A. 'A fox-covert study'. *J.E.*, **6** (1918) 110–25.
63 Pigott, C. D., and Taylor, K. 'The distribution of some woodland herbs in relation to the supply of nitrogen and phosphorus in the soil'. *J.E.*, **52** (*Suppl.*), 175–85.
64 *Winthrop Papers*, vol. I. Massachusetts Historical Society (1929).
65 Ault, W. O. *Open-field farming in medieval England.* Allen & Unwin (1972).
66 Anderson, M. D. *A saint at stake.* Faber (1964).
67 Supple, W. R. *A history of Thorpe-next-Norwich.* Norwich (1917).
68 Watson, C. E. 'The Minchinhampton custumal and its place in the story of the manor.' *Transactions of the Bristol and Gloucestershire Archaeological Society*, **54** (1932), 203–385.
69 Le Sueur, A. D. C. *Burnham Beeches.* Corporation of London (1955).
70 W. Suffolk R.O. 1066.
71 Another translation is published in W. Parker, *The history of Long Melford*, London (1873).
72 *Rotuli hundredorum*, H.M.S.O. (1810), vol. 1, p. 155.
73 P.R.O. E178/5297.
74 Liebermann, F. *Die Gesetze der Angelsachsen*, vol. 2. Halle (1906).
75 Essex R.O. D/DB T15/9.
76 *Cal. Close Rolls*, *temp.* Henry III *passim.*
77 Shorrocks, D. 'Hatfield Forest 1547–1857', *Essex Review*, **64** (1955), 54–66.
78 Hammersley, G. 'The Crown woods and their exploitation

in the sixteenth and seventeenth centuries'. *Bulletin of the Institute of Historical Research*, **30** (1957), 136–61.

79 P.R.O. LRRO/5/39.
80 Rose, F., and James, P. W. 'The corticolous and lignicolous species of the New Forest, Hampshire'. *Lichenologist*, **6** (1974) 1–72.
81 Clark, N. *Hadley Wood*. Ward Lock (1968).
82 *House of Commons Journal*.
83 Fisher, W. R. *The forest of Essex*. Butterworth (1887).
84 Tusser, T. *Fiue hundred pointes of good Husbandrie*. 1557.
85 M.C.O.R. 5382.
86 Eland, G. *At the courts of Great Canfield, Essex*. Oxford (1949).
87 Essex R.O. D/Dc E15/2.
88 E. Suffolk R.O. T1/1/16.
89 P.R.O. E178/3785, E178/4564, E178/4988.
90 Lobel, M. D. *Historic towns: Cambridge*. Scolar Press (1974).
91 Essex R.O. D/DHt M145.
92 Hervey, J. (ed.) *Ickworth Survey Boocke Ano 1665*.
93 Locke, G. M. *Census of woodlands 1965–67*. H.M.S.O. (1970).
94 Southgate, G. J. 'Helicopter spraying to kill overhead cover at Lavenham Forest, Suffolk'. *Journal of the Forestry Commission* **36**, (1969).
95 *New Scientist*, 6 March 1975.

Index and Glossary

This is intended to provide a glossary to this book; it does not include a general dictionary of woodland terms. Entries in capitals are ancient terms which in this book are used in more or less their traditional meaning. Words in italics (except Latin names of plants) are cross-references to other entries. Numbers in bold type refer to pages on which terms are dealt with in more detail.

Index and Glossary

Norwich Cathedral, timber 75

Oak, bog 45
    caterpillars 29, 106
    competition 33, 83, 102
    longevity 26–7, 158
    mildew 105
    numbers of, 76, 85, 102
    prehistory 40–3, 45, 48
    sizes of, 65, 75–6, 148
    two species 35, 128
    underwood 17, 22, 80, 95
    variation 128
    and see *Timber*
Offa's Dyke, Herefordshire 58
Old Buckenham, Norfolk 52
'Old-woodland' plants and animals 120, 125, 150
Overhall Grove, Boxworth, W. Cambs 130
Oxlip 83, 123–5, 130

PALE: deer-proof fence round the perimeter of a *park*. 144, 150
PANNAGE: fattening of domestic pigs under trees when there is a crop of *mast*. See *Swine (tame)*
Paris, Herb 125
Parish boundaries see *Boundaries*
PARK: area of land, consisting usually of *wood-pasture* at least in part, enclosed by a *pale* (distinction from *Forest* (b)), and intended for keeping deer. For other meanings see Chapter 8. 23–4, Figs. 14 and 15, 114, 142–151, Figs. 25 and 26, Plate XI
Park-bank 115, Fig. 20, 150
Pear 54
PERAMBULATION: legal document defining a piece of land by describing its boundaries. 49, 53, 159

Phosphate 129–30
Picea spp. see *Spruce*
Pig see *Swine*
PIGHTLE: small enclosure, especially attached to a house. 165
Pine, Scots 20, 35, 40, 45, 47, 94
Pinus pinaster 19
P. sylvestris see *Pine, Scots*
Pits 119, 134
Place-names 55–8, 108–9
PLAIN: part of a *Forest* sense (b) having few or no trees. 146, 152, 157, Fig. 27, 163
Plane (*Platanus* spp.) 19
Planned Countryside: districts whose landscape was reorganized during the post-1700 *enclosure movement*. Fig. 1, **17–18**, 114, 166, 168
PLANTATION: closely spaced stand of trees, other than an orchard, formed by planting them. 105, and see *Forestry*
Planting 96, 98, 121–2, 127–9, 132, 156, 181
    of hedges 166–7
    of hedgerow trees 170, 178
Plants as historical indicators 123–126
Poaching 155
POLLARD: tree which is cut at 8–12 ft above ground-level and allowed to grow again from the *bolling* to produce successive crops of *wood*. **Fig. 2, 22–3,** 29, Fig. 5, 34–5, 46, 54, 181, Plates VIII, X, XII
    on commons 138–41
    in Forests 152, 155–7, 160–5
    in hedges see *Hedgerow trees*
    longevity 24, 26–7
    in parks 142, 145–50